QUEEN OF HEAVEN

MARY'S BATTLE FOR SOULS

Brian Kennelly & Rick Rotondi

TAN Books
Charlotte, North Carolina

Cover and interior design by David Ferris Design

ISBN: 978-1-5051-0978-8

Published in the United States by
Saint Benedict Press
PO Box 410487
Charlotte, NC 28241

www.SaintBenedictPress.com

Printed in the United States of America

RIGHT
A common theme of Marian art is the Coronation of the Virgin, showing Mary honored by the heavenly host.

To the Queen of Heaven

Mother of mercy and
most gracious advocate

Who is she
that comes forth as
the morning rising,
fair as the moon,
bright as the sun,
terrible as an army
set in battle array?

CONTENTS

INTRODUCTION

There are only four doctrines that the Catholic Church holds definitively about Mary: She is the Mother of God; she conceived Jesus through the Holy Spirit and remained a virgin her entire life; she was free of all sin, personal and original, from the first instant of her conception; and at the end of her life, she was assumed body and soul into heaven. Profess these, and you profess all that the Church requires of her members regarding Mary.

Yet the place of Mary in the life of the Church is far richer than that. *De Maria numquam satis* goes an old Catholic saying: "Of Mary, there is never enough!" From the very beginning, starting even during the public ministry of Our Lord, the faithful have been drawn to contemplate the special status of his mother.

Theologians have explored and debated many propositions about Mary: her precise place in the divine economy, her role in distributing grace, whether or not she experienced death before her assumption into heaven. Scripture scholars, too, have been fascinated by Mary. They have pored over the relatively few Bible verses that mention her, discovering layers of insight and meaning. And of course in the heroic women of the Old Testament, and even in objects such as the Ark of the Covenant or the *hortus conclusus* ("enclosed garden") of the Song of Songs, they have seen Mary hinted at and foreshadowed.

Throughout history, a number of holy souls and mystics have claimed private revelations from Mary. Often these expand upon what is known of her life from the Bible, filling in the gaps and giving a glimpse of the things Luke tells us Mary pondered and kept in her heart (see Lk 2:19). And in a few extraordinary cases, credible witnesses claim to have been visited by Mary, who appears bodily to them with a message for a region, country, or all mankind.

While the Church never makes such apparitions a matter of faith, she has declared some "worthy of belief." Among these, three stand out, all commemorated on the Church's universal liturgical calendar: the apparitions at Guadalupe, Lourdes, and most recently Fatima, the one hundredth anniversary of which we celebrate this year.

Queen of Heaven is an exploration of the rich Catholic tradition about Mary, a synthesis of the writings of saints, Scripture scholars, mystics, and visionaries to tell the story of Mary from before time until today. We have drawn only from sources approved by the Church. With regard to theological speculations, most scriptural exegeses, and private revelations, Church approval is not a declaration of certain truth but rather a confirmation that the writings are not contrary to the Faith and may be held. This is all that we claim for our "eternal biography" of Mary; and here, as elsewhere, we submit in every matter to the judgment of the Church.

Queen of Heaven is not only the story of Mary. It is also the story of her great antagonist in the drama of salvation: the fallen angel who screamed no to God's plan in contrast to Mary's yes, the serpent who strikes at her offspring, the dragon who is enraged by her and seeks to devour her child (see Rv 12:4). In brief, *Queen of Heaven* is about the battle for souls waged between Mary and the devil; and because the Church is even more circumspect in its teaching about the devil than about Mary, virtually everything we posit about his activities in history is a matter of speculation, too.

The *Catechism of the Catholic Church* tells us that the devil has "a disastrous influence," that he "may act in the world out of hatred for God and his kingdom in Christ Jesus," and that "his action may cause grave injuries—of a spiritual nature and, indirectly, even of a physical nature" (CCC 394–395). Yet specifying exactly what injurious events in history are due to the devil's actions or influence, rather than unaided human weakness or malice, is a task the Church almost always declines. Atrocities such as the human sacrifice of the Aztecs, the sacrileges of the French Revolution, and the gulags of the Soviets were diabolical at least in the figurative sense. Were they directly inspired by the devil? In the end, that is more than we can say definitively. But we can suspect, and do so in good company, as you will soon come to see.

A final note about the role of Mary in God's plan. Though Mary's glories are so great that they can hardly be exaggerated—though in her praise enough can never be said—she is still the

ABOVE
The fall of the rebel angels as described in Revelation 12:7-9.

3

handmaid of the Lord, as well as queen, who points not at herself but at her Son, telling one and all to "do whatever he tells you" (Jn 2:5).

In the game of chess, it is the king who rules the board, the one who determines the fate of the game. But it is the queen who, at the king's willing, flies about protecting her subjects from the enemy. As we will attempt to show, our queen, the Queen of Heaven, has done just this for the last two millennia. She has left her throne and returned to defend her children time and time again. She has come to lead us back to the kingdom so that we may fall in adoration before the King.

February 11, 2017
Feast of Our Lady of Lourdes

LEFT
At Cana, Mary told the servers "do whatever he tells you" (Jn 2:5).

RIGHT
The Magi were among the first adorers of the King.

The Battle Begins

CHAPTER

1

The Queen of Heaven was born just over two thousand years ago, coming of age in the little village of Nazareth in Galilee. But Mary's story begins well before that; in fact, before time itself.

The great evangelist Archbishop Fulton Sheen said we can picture Mary as being with God, existing as an eternal thought in the divine mind, not only at creation, but before it. In the dedication to his famous book about Mary, *The World's First Love*, Sheen called Mary "the Woman whom even God dreamed of before the world was made."

Sheen's observation is echoed in *Lumen Gentium*, one of the principal documents of the Second Vatican Council, and in the *Catechism of the Catholic Church*. *Lumen Gentium* refers to Mary as the predestined mother (see LG 56), while the *Catechism* teaches that "from all eternity," God chose Mary to be the mother of his Son (CCC 488).

Knowing God's eternal plan for Mary helps us understand her role in the economy of salvation. It also sheds light on the enmity that would arise between her and the prince of darkness.

The prince of darkness. Yes . . . he is a reality. From the very beginning, he has also taken part in the cosmic drama of our salvation. And in understanding his origins and his revolt at the dawn of creation, we can better understand Our Lady and the role she plays in the battle for souls.

WAR IN HEAVEN

God existed eternally, before any of his creations. His existence was not a solitary one, for there was the Father, the Son, and the Holy Spirit, living in a communion of indescribable love. Despite having no need to share that love outside the Trinity, God willed to do so.

He began with the creation of the angels. God created them good, but just as he would do with us, he gave the angels free will. Only free creatures can truly love; a compulsory love is no love at all.

Much about the angels remains a mystery. We know they are powerful, immortal. We know God created a great multitude or host. And we know that some of them abused their free will, rebelled against God, and so became devils.

Tradition calls the leader of the rebel angels Lucifer, which means "Day Star." The name is taken from Isaiah:

> *How you are fallen from heaven,*
> *O Day Star, son of Dawn!*
> *How you are cut down to the ground,*
> *you who laid the nations low!*
> *You said in your heart,*
> *'I will ascend to heaven;*
> *above the stars of God*
> *I will set my throne on high;*
> *I will sit on the mount of assembly*
> *in the far north;*
> *I will ascend above the heights of the clouds,*
> *I will make myself like the Most High.'*

(Is 14:12–14)

While Isaiah was speaking directly to an ancient king of Babylon, the Church has long seen in his words a deeper meaning: a reference to the devil and his rebellious desire to dethrone God. Lucifer's mutiny was quelled, and he was cast from heaven; thus, Isaiah continues, "But you are brought down to Sheol, to the depths of the Pit" (14:15).

The devil's expulsion from heaven is further expanded on in Revelation:

> Now war arose in heaven, Michael and his angels fighting against the dragon; and the dragon and his angels fought, but they were defeated and there was no longer any place for them in heaven. And the great dragon was thrown down, that ancient serpent, who is called the Devil and Satan, the deceiver of the whole world—he was thrown to the earth, and his angels were thrown down with him. (Rv 12:7–9)

Lucifer and his rebel angels responded, *"Non serviam"* ("I will not serve").

Before he was cast from heaven, Lucifer was likely the mightiest angel of all. Michael, whose name means "Who is like God," was of a lower rank. But unlike Lucifer, Michael burned for God's glory. With the other faithful angels by his side, he won this famous battle in heaven, hurling Lucifer and his cohorts to earth.

What prompted Lucifer to launch his doomed rebellion? The traditional answer is pride. "Pride goes before destruction, and a haughty spirit before a fall," the Bible's Book of Proverbs tells us (16:18). And we have already seen how Isaiah associates the fall of the Day Star with pride, his determination to "make myself like the Most High."

Yet this begs the question: How could the most intelligent of creatures be so foolish as to desire freedom from his own Creator? Lucifer was smart enough to know he could never replace or dethrone God, that it was God who sustains him in being moment by moment. For an angel, or any creature, to revolt against God is as nonsensical as a sunbeam desiring to exist apart from the sun.

This question of what *precisely* riled Lucifer's pride and prompted his revolt is a great mystery.

The *Catechism* says simply that the fall of the devil and the angels who joined him consisted in their free and irrevocable choice to reject God and his reign (see CCC 392). Anything beyond this is speculation. What we know is that, asked to serve, Lucifer and his rebel angels responded, *"Non serviam"* ("I will not serve").

But in examining the writings of the saints and Church Fathers, one possible answer appears again and again for why Lucifer might have incited a mutiny in heaven. It is this answer that brings our Queen into the fray.

GOD'S PLAN FOR CREATION

We have said that Mary is the woman whom "God dreamed of before the world was made." Before he created the angels, before he created anything, God had Mary in mind. Why?

Because from all eternity, he planned the Incarnation. From all eternity, God willed that the Word become flesh. And this would happen through Mary, through her *fiat*, her yes.

Does this mean the Incarnation would have occurred even if our first parents had never fallen? Would Jesus have come even if we had never sinned?

The Church leaves this question unsettled, and theologians have differed. Some have held that although God planned the Incarnation from eternity, he did so only because he foresaw the Fall and wished to rescue us from it.

But the *Catechism* gives several reasons for the Incarnation in addition to our redemption through Christ's death on the Cross. Christ also came so that we might know God's love, so that we would have a model for holiness, and, finally, so that we might be partakers in the divine nature itself (see CCC 457–460).

None of these other reasons presuppose the Fall; they align more with the famous quote of St. Athanasius, one of the first Doctors of the Church, who said, "the Son of God became man so that we might become God"—that is, come to share, in a limited way, in God's very own life.

Many saints have taught that God's desire to unite himself with us is the fundamental reason for the Incarnation. These saints include St. Albert the Great, St. Maximus the Confessor, and St. Francis de Sales. Blessed John Duns Scotus is the theologian most known for championing this position. St. John Paul II beatified Duns Scotus in 1993, praising him as a "minstrel of the Incarnation." And Pope Benedict XVI praised him as well:

> Unlike many Christian thinkers of the time, [Duns Scotus] held that the Son of God would have been made man even if humanity had not sinned. . . . This perhaps somewhat surprising thought crystallized because, in the opinion of Duns Scotus the Incarnation of the Son of God, planned from all eternity by God the Father at the level of love is the fulfilment of creation and enables every creature, in Christ and through Christ, to be filled with grace and to praise and glorify God in eternity. Although Duns Scotus was aware that in fact, because of original sin, Christ redeemed us with his Passion, Death and Resurrection, he reaffirmed that the Incarnation is the greatest and most beautiful work of the entire history of salvation, that it is not conditioned by any contingent fact but is **God's original idea of ultimately uniting with himself the whole of creation, in the Person and Flesh of the Son.** (Benedict XVI, General Audience of July 7, 2010, emphasis added)

In *The Mystical City of God,* Ven. Maria of Agreda writes that the rebellion of Lucifer, the great dragon, was prompted by God disclosing to the angels his plan for the Incarnation.

MARIA OF AGREDA ON LUCIFER'S FALL

Maria of Agreda was a seventeenth-century Spanish nun who received spiritual revelations about Mary and Jesus, which are recorded in *The Mystical City of God*. Private revelations such as Agreda's are never binding on the faithful and must be measured against the public or official revelation of the Church. But they are often the fruit of special graces to saintly individuals. And Maria certainly appears to have been saintly. She was declared venerable by the Church shortly after her death, and her body remains incorrupt to this day.

One of Maria's revelations concerns the fall of Lucifer. At the dawn of creation, writes Maria, the angels were given three visions. First, God disclosed to them his own divine nature as Trinity: Father, Son, and Holy Spirit. All the angels worshipped him—though Lucifer did so out of duty rather than joy.

In the second vision, God revealed that he intended to create men and women, formed from the dust of the earth. The second person of the Trinity, the Son, would take their flesh, and the angels were to worship the God-man.

Finally, God showed the angels that his Son would become incarnate by a Woman, and they were to honor her as their Queen.

On being shown the second and third visions, Lucifer was furious. He refused to adore the God-man and venerate the Queen. As Maria tells it, "He vowed to tear down the plan God had set in motion, persecuting and destroying this race of creatures God so cherished. He cried out with hatred at mankind and at the woman whom God had raised up, declaring that he would battle her until the end of the ages."

And yet God had the last word. *This Woman you refuse to honor shall crush your head*, the Lord responded. *And if, through your pride, death enters the world, life and salvation shall enter through her humility.*

Duns Scotus's thought may have been surprising at the time, but it should not have been. His insight goes all the way back to St. Paul, who calls Christ "the first-born of all creation" and says, "He is before all things, and in him all things hold together" (Col 1:15, 17).

THE GREAT TEST

With these reflections on God's plan for creation, we are better prepared to understand what many saints, Fathers, and mystics believed was the reason for the rebellion of Lucifer and his angels: that God revealed his plan for the Incarnation to them, and they in turn refused to worship the incarnate Son, Christ Jesus. Not only this, they refused to venerate the Woman who would give the Word flesh, the Woman who would become their Queen.

In his book *The Screwtape Letters,* which is a fictional correspondence between two devils, C. S. Lewis has Lucifer (whom Screwtape calls "Our Father") reacting in disgust when God ("the Enemy") reveals his plan to create men and women and draw them into his love.

"Humans," writes Screwtape, "are amphibians—half spirit and half animal. (The Enemy's determination to produce such a revolting hybrid was one of the things that determined Our Father to withdraw his support from Him.)"[1]

An earlier and very influential work, *The Mystical City of God,* written by Maria of Agreda, a seventeenth-century Franciscan nun, makes the same point in more detail. At the beginning of time, Maria says, God gave the angels a great test. He revealed to them his plan for the Incarnation and asked the angels to worship the God-man as their Lord. The good angels did so and were rewarded with eternal bliss. But Lucifer and his angels were filled with rage and jealousy and refused. "In disorderly fury [Lucifer] aspired to be himself the head of all the human race," says Agreda, adding that if God were to unite himself with another nature, Lucifer "demanded that it be consummated in him."

LEFT
Fulton Sheen called Mary "the Woman whom even God dreamed of before the world was made."

---

[1] C. S. Lewis, *The Screwtape Letters* (San Francisco: Harper, 2001), p. 37.

Both Lewis and Agreda are reflecting a tradition with very strong roots, stretching back through saints and Fathers to Scripture itself. Many scholars, for example, have seen a reference to the test of the angels in this passage from the Letter to the Hebrews: "And again, when he brings the first-born into the world, he says, 'Let all God's angels worship him'" (Heb 1:6).

The twelfth chapter of Revelation provides what may be another hint of the angelic test. John describes a fascinating vision: A woman clothed with the sun, with the moon under her feet and a crown of stars on her head, about to give birth. Suddenly, a great red dragon appears beside her. The dragon sweeps a third of the stars from the sky. Then he prepares to devour the woman's child when she gives birth (see Rev 12:1–4).

The timing and ordering of this passage are striking. Here we have a vision directly from Sacred Scripture that associates, at least through symbols, a revelation of the Incarnation (the woman about to give birth) with Lucifer (the great dragon) and the rebel angels (the one-third of the stars the dragon sweeps from the sky).

PRINCE OF THIS WORLD

Is this how the battle began, then? Did God reveal to the angels his plan to unite himself with the human race through the Woman? And did such a thought so offend Lucifer's pride that he incited a mutiny?

Whatever the answers to these fascinating questions, we know that the battle lines were drawn as Lucifer was cast like lightning from heaven (see Lk 10:18) to take up dominion on earth as prince of this world. There he slithered about as the serpent, the one we know as Satan. We will come to see clear evidence of his hatred for mankind, for the Woman, and for the Son she would bear. Soon we will hear the hissing of his deceitful tongue as we step into the Garden.

"The dragon stood before the woman who was about to bear a child, that he might devour her child when she brought it forth" (Rv 12:4).

The Woman and the Serpent

CHAPTER

2

LEFT
"I will put enmity you
and the woman"
(Gn 3:15).

Lucifer had been defeated, but his fight would rage on. He prowled throughout the world, seeking the ruin of the very species that would give flesh to the Incarnate Word. He would begin his attack by targeting the first woman, Eve.

Could it have been that the serpent thought this was the Woman, the one who would make possible the Incarnation? Did he think if he corrupted this woman, this mother of all the living, he might prevent the Incarnation? It might have been more fitting for him to approach Adam; after all, we know Adam was the first created human and the head of the race.

No matter his reasons, he slithered up to Eve first. The third chapter of Genesis tells us that the serpent beguiled her with a series of questions, feigning ignorance about what God had told her and Adam concerning the Tree of the Knowledge of Good and Evil.

"Did God say, 'You shall not eat of any tree of the garden'?" the serpent asked.

"We may eat of the fruit of the trees of the garden," came Eve's reply, "but God said, 'You shall not eat of the fruit of the tree which is in the midst of the garden, neither shall you touch it, lest you die.'"

"You will not die," said the serpent, his words dripping with mockery of God's warning. "God knows that when you eat of it your eyes will be opened and you will be like God, knowing good and evil."

Eve gazed upon the tree and saw it was good for food and a delight to the eyes. She felt it would make her wise, so she took the fruit and ate it before giving it to her husband as well.

Let us note that the tree in itself was a good thing, for all that God had made was good (see Gn 1:31). The sin came in Eve's choosing this good at the expense of a greater one—obeying God's command.

The consequences of this disobedience were devastating. The serpent had lied; Adam and Eve *would* die, forfeiting by their sin God's gift of freedom from corruption and decay. They had played out on their own stage in Eden the rebellion of Lucifer and his angels. Now they, too, would be cast from God's presence into a world ruled by the very one who had enticed them to sin.

And yet, unlike Lucifer, their choosing to sin was not irrevocable. Lucifer had scorned humanity as inferior to the angels, unworthy to be united with God through the Incarnation, but Adam and Eve's very inferiority allowed a ray of hope. They could not pour themselves fully into a single act as the angels could; they could repent; God could, if he chose, offer them a way out of the devil's dominion and back into his.

It's at this point in the story that God turns to the serpent and delivers one of the most well-known passages in all of Scripture:

> *Because you have done this,*
> *cursed are you above all cattle,*
> *and above all wild animals;*
> *upon your belly you shall go,*
> *and dust you shall eat*
> *all the days of your life.*
> *I will put enmity between you and the woman,*
> *and between your seed and her seed;*
> *he shall bruise your head,*
> *and you shall bruise his heel.*

(Gn 3:14–15)

Genesis 3:15 is what's known as the *protoevangelium,* or the "first gospel," because it is the first announcement of the coming of a Savior. God tells us here that he would put enmity between the serpent and a certain woman, a woman who's offspring (seed) would come to crush the serpent's head.

This, of course, refers to Mary and Jesus, to the aggression that would exist between Mary and the devil, and to Christ's ultimate victory that came through his crucifixion and resurrection. Christ's heel, a symbol of his humanity because it is how he walked upon the earth, would be bruised on the Cross. Yet it was precisely in this moment, and three days later at the Resurrection, that the serpent's head was crushed.

ENMITY WITH THE WOMAN

At Calvary, the serpent lost the war for humanity. But the battle continues because he can still win the war for our own souls. Though the evil one cannot defeat the head of the body, Christ, he can continue to strike at the heel of the body, humanity, and

does so to this day. This is why the *protoevangelium* can be viewed as a battle cry, a proclamation of war between the wicked and the good, and it is our Queen who leads us in this battle.

If we have any doubt about God's desire to make Mary a central figure in the battle, we must ask why he chose to mention her at this most pivotal moment in history. He could have made the battle solely between Jesus and the devil. Yet God explicitly introduced "the woman" to this battle and placed her at enmity with the prince of evil.

Note, too, that God says "*the* woman," not "*a* woman." Recall our speculation that the catalyst for Lucifer's rebellion was the revelation to the angels of the Incarnation and the woman who would give the Word flesh. By telling the serpent that he would put enmity between him and the woman, God appears to be referring to a specific woman—the one he had shown the devil at the dawn of time.

After our first parents were cast from the garden of Eden, the Old Testament reads as a chronicle of the devil's attacks on humanity. He inspired brother to kill brother; he corrupted the world so much that God had to wipe it clean with a catastrophic flood; he enticed the prideful construction of a tower that reached to the heavens; he led many astray in Egypt, Canaan, and Babylon through the worship of pagan gods; he tempted leaders like David; and the people that God had set apart, to prepare them for the coming of the Savior, he besieged again and again, not only with temptations to sin and idolatry, but with hostile armies, foreign captivity, civil war, and finally, brutal subjugation under the rule of the mighty Roman Empire.

Human frailty and disobedience and sin should be blamed for many of these calamities. But one cannot ignore the role the devil played in the corruption of the world. For one, he was the tempter who brought on the stain of original sin, which leads to humanity's frailty, disobedience, and lack of faith. But still, as Christ himself would say, Satan was "ruler of this world" (Jn 12:31; 14:30), and he had real (though limited) power in his dominion.

Amidst the devil's many victories, God pushed his plan of salvation forward, showering mercy upon his people even when they proved unworthy. And, at times, he gave us glimpses and hints of the Woman he had dreamt of since before time, the Woman who would come to conquer the evil prince by delivering a Savior and King.

THE PROMISE OF A QUEEN

A fundamental principle of Bible scholarship is the importance of reading the Old Testament in light of the New, and the New in light of the Old. While we can discover the *literal sense* of Scripture by reading the text of a passage itself, understanding the *spiritual sense*, in all its layers, requires familiarity with connections and threads between passages from different books of the Bible.

A *type* is one example of these threads that connects the Old and New Testaments. A type is a person, thing, or event in the old covenant, or Old Testament, that prepares for or foreshadows the new covenant, or something in the New Testament.

During the long millennia between the fall of Adam and the arrival of the Savior, God encouraged his people with many types or foreshadowings of Mary. For example, the Old Testament tells us of several barren women, such as Sarah and Hannah, miraculously giving birth to great leaders of God's people. Mary is the fulfillment of this type: not a barren woman, but a virgin who miraculously gives birth to God himself.

Other Old Testament heroines foreshadow Mary because of their actions in defeating evil. For example, Jael drives a tent peg through the temple of Sisera, the enemy general of the Canaanite army (see Jgs 4:21), and Judith cuts off the head of Holofernes, the Assyrian general (see Jdt 13:8). Note that in both of these instances, the enemy's head is targeted, just as the serpent's is in the *protoevangelium*.

Another example is Esther, who helped hang Haman, a vizier in the Persian Empire (see Est 7:10). This triumph of a delicate and unprepossessing female over a mighty and evil enemy anticipates Mary's victory over the devil.

And finally, think of the mother of the seven brothers in Maccabees who is forced to watch the torture and martyrdom of her sons (see 2 Mc 7). We see in her a direct foreshadowing of Mary as the sorrowful mother, standing at the foot of the Cross.

Another foreshadowing of Mary in the Old Testament is the queen mother. Though we most often think of a queen as the king's wife, this was not the case in the Davidic Kingdom. Since the royal kings of Israel and the House of David had so many wives, no single wife had the influence that the king's mother enjoyed.

When Solomon brought out a throne, placing a seat of power at his right, it was for his mother, and when she asks him for a favor, he says he cannot refuse her (see 1 Kgs 2:19–20). Solomon's

Detail from *The Last Judgement* by Fra Angelico showing an ape-like Satan devouring the damned in hell. The devil is often depicted as an ape in religious art, one who mimics and mocks the way God relates to men.

THE APE OF GOD

Diabolus simia Dei. It's an expression coined in the Middle Ages but common to the thinking of the Church Fathers. It means "the devil is the ape of God."

The devil's pride and envy drive him to make himself like the Most High (see Is 14:14) to mimic and mock the way God relates to men. It is a vain attempt to disrupt God's plan for creation, a monstrous effort to place himself at the center of all things.

The Bible records many ways the devil mocked and aped God in the generations after the Fall. Two stand out: his incitement of idolatry and of sexual immorality.

Idolatry is the worship of pagan gods. While it's common today to dismiss these gods as figments of the imagination, that is not the view of Scripture or the Fathers. "What pagans sacrifice they offer to demons," says St. Paul (1 Cor 10:20). The widespread pagan worship of antiquity was not made to a void; it was made to—and solicited by—fallen angels, hungry to receive for themselves the worship they had refused to give to Christ.

Sexual immorality was closely associated with idolatry, which often incorporated rituals involving temple prostitution as well as child sacrifice. Why would demons inspire and foment such practices? Perhaps to express their hatred of the Incarnation. Marriage, says St. Paul, is a great sign or type of God uniting with humanity, of Christ's union with the Church (see Eph 5:31–32). Sexual immorality makes a mockery of marriage, obscuring and attacking God's plan for creation—his desire to unite himself with man.

actions here point to a time when another Son of David, Jesus, will sit on the throne. His Queen, too, will sit by his side, and when she intercedes with him for her children, he too will not refuse.

THE NEW ARK

Perhaps the most prominent foreshadowing of Mary in the Old Testament is the Ark of the Covenant. In the Book of Exodus, God commands Moses to construct the Ark. The Ark would become the most sacred object on earth because it served as the dwelling place of God. For a time it was housed in the tabernacle, a kind of portable shrine or tent built especially for the Ark. Later, Solomon would build a temple and the Ark would be housed there.

The connections between the Ark and Mary are many. Consider first the description in Exodus of how the presence of God came to dwell in the Ark after Moses consecrated it: "Then the cloud covered the tent of meeting, and the glory of the LORD filled the tabernacle" (Ex 40:34). When the Archangel Gabriel tells Mary how she will come to bear the Son of God, his language is remarkably similar: "The Holy Spirit will come upon you, and the power of the Most High will overshadow you" (Lk 1:35).

Consider also what was within the Ark. It contained the tablets of the law which were God's word, the manna (or bread) the Israelites ate while wandering in the desert, and Aaron's rod that miraculously budded, representing the high priesthood (see Heb 9:4). These sacred objects point to what Mary, the New Ark, would contain in carrying Christ. For Christ is the Word of God, not in stone, but in the flesh; he is the Bread of Life; and he is the High Priest. Finally we arrive at yet another foreshadowing of Mary in the Song of Solomon: "Who is this that looks forth like the dawn, fair as the moon, bright as the sun, terrible as an army with banners?" (see Sg 6:10). The Church has long applied these words to Mary. She is like the dawn because she signifies the coming of a new day, bringing with her the Light of the world, and Revelation

LEFT
Mary is the New Ark who bore God himself in her womb.

tells us she is bright as the sun because she is clothed in it and fair as the moon because it rests below her feet (see Rv 12:1). And she is terrible as an army because she is that Woman who, from the beginning, has been prepared for battle with the serpent.

Since his no to God's plan for creation, since his rebellion and his refusal to serve, Lucifer had devoted his existence to our corruption. Our Lord called Satan "a murderer from the beginning" (Jn 8:44). A murderer who hates men and women made in the image and likeness of God. A murderer who could not bear—and would do all in his power to prevent—God's coming to take flesh through the predestined mother.

His victories mounted and his confidence grew. It seemed nothing would interrupt his dominion over us. But God had not forgotten his promise in the Garden, his promise that the serpent would be crushed. Though for many generations he sent only glimpses and foreshadowings of the Woman, he would, in the fullness of time, when the power of the serpent might have seemed at its peak, send the Angel Gabriel to a home in Nazareth, to the Woman who was full of grace.

ABOVE
Satan, whom Our Lord called "a murderer from the beginning" (Jn 8:44), led Cain to murder his brother Abel.

RIGHT
God did not forgot his promise in the Garden, that the serpent would be crushed.

The Day Creation Held Its Breath

⬦

CHAPTER

3

Most of the great events of history occur in public places and before throngs of people—on battlefields, in palaces and government chambers, or amidst the streets of large cities. But one of the greatest, most dramatic events in history occurred in a forgotten village, in the presence of no one save an angel of God and a virgin, a young girl unknown to the world at the time.

This event, the Annunciation, is the day of the Incarnation, the day the Word became flesh. It is the day that split history in two—*AD* and *BC*—the day all creation held its breath.

And how silently, how softly, it came. One of the great poems of the Middle Ages, titled *I Sing of a Maiden,* says that Christ came to Mary as still "as dew in April / that falls on the grass."

The still and hidden nature of the Incarnation reveals the great humility of Mary, as well as the humility of Our Lord; not only this, it reveals his wisdom. For by coming to us in so humble a way, he would, for a time, evade the notice of the devil, who had lain in wait for precisely this moment: the moment the God-man would arrive.

HANDMAID OF THE LORD

Mary came from Nazareth, a village so humble that the Apostle Nathaniel once asked if anything good could possibly come out of it (see Jn 1:46). Nazareth was a place where simple people lived. It was not Rome, nor Athens, nor Jerusalem. While Joseph was descended from the House of David, we have no evidence that Mary herself shared this royal bloodline. In the *Magnificat,* Mary refers to herself as lowly and calls herself, not a queen, but a servant—the handmaid of the Lord (see Lk 1:46–55).

Tradition tells us that Mary was presented at the Temple at a young age and consecrated to God. She gave herself entirely to him. Father Marie-Dominique Philippe, a well-respected Dominican theologian and author, argued in his book *The Mysteries of Mary* that this was the perfect way for Mary to hide from the devil. Fr. Philippe wrote, "This consecration of abandonment is the best way for Mary to strengthen herself in God against the attacks of the devil. For in abandoning herself to the Father's mercy, she hides in this mercy and escapes the devil's notice. She flees into the desert. Satan knows nothing about Mary's first gesture. This is the first way Mary crushes Satan's head!"[2]

It's good to pause here and reflect on just how Mary was able to evade the devil's notice, at least for a time. The devil was perhaps the mightiest angel God had created, with legions of demons at his command. His ability to scour the world for the God-man and his mother was unmatched. And his compulsion to find them, mock them, and stop or disrupt them must have been unsleeping.

If the devil did not see Mary, it was because her humility shielded her from his eyes. He knew the Woman's place in creation as Mother of God; he knew the throne she would sit on; he had desired it for himself.

What he could not understand is that the Woman would be not only God's preeminent creature but his most humble one as well. He looked for the Woman; but he did not expect to find her

---

[2] Fr. Marie-Dominique Philippe, OP, *The Mysteries of Mary: Growing in Faith, Hope, and Love with the Mother of God* (Charlotte, NC: TAN Books, 2011), p. 64.

in Nazareth, and he could not fathom that she would be a simple handmaid. For the devil, it would be a catastrophic error.

THE TURNING POINT

The great poet Dante Alighieri in his masterpiece *The Divine Comedy* pays tribute to Mary by calling her the "predestined turning point of God's intention" (*Paradiso*, Canto 33).

The *turning point:* there is perhaps no better way to describe the Annunciation. At the beginning of human history, through the corruption of Eve, the devil turned our trajectory away from God and toward sin, misery, and death. At the Annunciation, Mary turned us back.

Chronologically, the Annunciation is one of the first events of the New Testament. One of the first events of the Old is the

ABOVE
Eve's choice to eat of the forbidden fruit was the primal disaster that brought death into our world.

Fall. It is the first of many parallels between these two most critical moments in salvation history.

In Eden, three characters are present: Eve, Adam, and the serpent, a fallen angel. At the Annunciation, there are also three characters: the new Eve, the new Adam, and an archangel. While the fallen angel comes to Eve with a message of death, the archangel comes to Mary with a message of life.

Consider also the similarities between Eve and Mary. Both are virgins, sinless, and free. Both will become mothers of a new people; they will each be "Mother of All" in their own spheres; that is, "Mother of All the Living" and "Mother of All Who Live in Christ." Lastly, both are faced with a choice regarding fruit and a tree, and for each, their choice will affect every person throughout history.

But there the similarities end.

Eve's choice to disobey God and eat the fruit of the Tree of the Knowledge of Good and Evil is the primal disaster. When Adam ratifies her choice, they lose, for themselves and all humanity, the great gifts with which God had endowed them: friendship with him, freedom from death, untroubled dominion over themselves and creation.

Conversely, Mary's choice to obey God and bear Jesus as the fruit of her womb is the beginning of our salvation. That salvation will not be won until a day in the future, when Mary will stand beneath another tree, the Cross, with Jesus as he pours out his life for the life of the world. But her yes to God makes salvation possible and anticipates the moment when Jesus will restore man's friendship with God and offer eternal life to all who want it.

At the Annunciation, Mary reverses the fall of Eve and begins to undo the tangle she had brought to human nature. "And so it was that the knot of Eve's disobedience was loosed by Mary's obedience," said St. Irenaeus. "For what the virgin bound fast by her refusal to believe, the Virgin Mary unbound by her belief" (*Against Heresies* III, 22, 34).

Blessed John Henry Newman also spoke of this reversal sparked by Mary at the Annunciation. In his sermon "The Glories of Mary for the Sake of Her Son," he preached, "The course of ages was to be reversed; the tradition of evil was to be broken; a gate of light was to be opened amid the darkness, for the coming of the Just: a Virgin conceived and bore Him."

This insight of the Annunciation reversing Eve's devastating choice is not something contemplated only by theologians and saints. It is a truth that has been recognized and celebrated at a popular level in feast, prayer, and song. It is reflected in one of the most beautiful devotional titles for Our Lady, Cause of Our Joy—a contrast to Eve, cause of all our woe. And it is found in the popular folk songs of the Middle Ages such as *Ave fit ex Eva,* which delight in pointing out that the first word of the Hail Mary in Latin *(Ave)* is the reverse of the word for Eve *(Eva).*

ABOVE
Dante called the Annunciation the "turning point" of salvation history.

40

THE WOMAN WHO SAID YES . . . AND THE ANGEL WHO SAID NO

The Annunciation reversed and overturned the disaster at the beginning of history: the fall of Eve. But it also answered another fall, one that was earlier, before human history, and more devastating still: the fall of Lucifer.

Recall the speculation we have discussed previously: It was God's revelation of his plan for the Incarnation that prompted Lucifer's rebellion. He revealed this plan to Mary at Nazareth just over two thousand years ago. It was then that he shared with her what he had shown to the angels eons before.

The angels had their moment when God approached and asked them to accept the incarnation of his Son—and the course of salvation history hung in the balance. The good angels welcomed God's plan for the Incarnation with humility and joy. And God had immediately rewarded them for it, welcoming them in turn into the fullness of heaven, sharing with them his own divine life.

Lucifer's response was different. He was the mightiest of God's creatures, and in his overweening pride, he could not bear the thought that he should be supplanted by another. When asked if he would accept the Incarnation, he had shouted no.

Lucifer's rebellion had not only led to his own expulsion from heaven but also ruptured the unity of God's creation, rent it in two. Whereas before, all in creation had been light, now there was darkness.

Lucifer had challenged the goodness and justice of God's plan and had to be answered. And he would be—ultimately by Christ, who, though of a station infinitely above Lucifer's, did not scorn to take the form of a servant, and who said yes to God's plan even to the point of accepting death on the Cross (see Phil 2:5–8).

But Lucifer was answered by Mary as well. When God asks Mary to consent to his plan for the Incarnation, she replies yes.

At the Annunciation, all creation held its breath in anticipation of Mary's reply to the archangel Gabriel, for her consent to bear the promised Savior and become the Mother of God.

RANSOM FOR THE CAPTIVE

The devil has a certain dominion over us because of Adam's fall. The devil presides, in the words of the Council of Trent, over "the empire of death." We are born captives of his empire due to original sin.

For long centuries, men and women suffered this captivity without relief. Yet from the beginning, God had a plan to ransom us—a plan which required Mary's consent. St. Bernard of Clairvaux conveys the drama of this moment and the scope of what is at stake in this excerpt from his sermon on the Annunciation:

> O Virgin, . . . the angel awaits an answer; it is time for him to return to God. We too are waiting, O Lady, for your word of compassion. . . . We shall be set free at once if you consent. . . . Tearful Adam with his sorrowing family begs this of you in their exile from Paradise. Abraham begs it, David begs it. All the other holy patriarchs, your ancestors, ask it of you, as they dwell in the country of the shadow of death. This is what the whole earth waits for, prostrate at your feet. It is right in doing so, for on your word depends comfort for the wretched, ransom for the captive, freedom for the condemned, indeed, salvation for all the sons of Adam, the whole of your race. Answer quickly, O Virgin. . . . Answer with a word, receive the Word of God. Speak your own word, conceive the divine Word. Breathe a passing word, embrace the eternal Word. . . . And behold the handmaid of the Lord, she says be it done unto me according to Thy word.

Fiat, she says, in the Latin translation of Luke's account of the Annunciation. *Let it be done to me according to your word.*

A short time later, Mary goes on to recite her famous canticle, the Magnificat. It is a hymn of praise to God, but it is also a rebuke to those who oppose him.

> *The Mighty One has done great things for me,*
> *and holy is his name.*
> *His mercy is from age to age*
> *to those who fear him.*
> *He has shown might with his arm,*
> *dispersed the arrogant of mind and heart.*
> *He has thrown down the rulers from their thrones*
> *but lifted up the lowly.*

(Lk 1:49–52 NABRE)

Of all rulers who have been thrown from their thrones, none was mightier, or fell more spectacularly, than Lucifer. Conversely, no creature has been raised higher than Mary. Both Lucifer and Mary show in their own sphere the truth of Christ's statement, "Whoever exalts himself will be humbled, and whoever humbles himself will be exalted" (Mt 23:12).

In the providence of God, Mary's *fiat* at the Annunciation is a reversal of Eve's fall and an example of perfect discipleship to us, of "hearing the word of God and obeying it" (see Lk 11:28). But it is something more still. It is an answer to the one who shouted, *"Non serviam!"* at the dawn of creation. It is a rebuke to and humiliation of the devil, not through force of arms, not through the simple exercise of omnipotence, but through goodness, holiness, and humility.

The great St. Louis de Montfort wrote in his spiritual classic *True Devotion to Mary* that "what Lucifer has lost by pride, Mary has gained by humility." This dynamic unfolds across all salvation history in their enmity and opposition, but nowhere was it more evident than at the Annunciation.

LEFT
No creature has been raised higher than Mary.

MODEL OF HUMILITY

Mary was truly God's masterpiece, his most perfect creation. She was the Queen of his kingdom and the mother of all who would live in him. She was the perfect model of humility and virtue and the first disciple of Christ. And she was the one through whom he would crush the serpent, who had corrupted the first woman in an attempt to obstruct God's plan for creation.

For generations, Lucifer had reigned as prince of this world. But in his pride, he had failed to discover the humble handmaid who would deliver the promised Savior. In his arrogance, fed by so many past victories, he could not imagine that the Queen whose Son would crush him would be a young girl from the little village of Nazareth.

But as we will see, this simple girl, before winning her victory and assuming her queenship, would have to endure profound sorrow. Soon she would feel the blade of a sword pierce through her immaculate heart.

RIGHT
Mary was the perfect model of humility and virtue and the first disciple of Christ.

The Sorrowful Mother

CHAPTER

4

Mary is mentioned only a handful of times in
the Bible. She speaks even less. Perhaps it is for this reason that
John Lynch called her "the woman wrapped in silence" in his
epic poem of this name. But when we do encounter her, we cannot help but notice a recurring, and surprising, theme: After the
great triumph of the Annunciation, she quickly becomes a woman
well-acquainted with sorrow.

St. Alphonsus Ligouri writes in *The Glories of Mary* that "God
willed her to be the Queen of Sorrows. . . . She always had to
see before her eyes, and continually to suffer, all the torments that
awaited her." It's common to picture Mary only at the foot of the
Cross when we think of her as Our Lady of Sorrows, but in fact,
her heart felt the heaviness of human sorrow from the very beginning of her long path to Golgotha.

Just like with our own trials, Mary's suffering had a purpose.
But let us first chronicle her sorrowful path before we reveal the
divine workings of God's plan for the Mother of the Church.

A SWORD WILL PIERCE YOUR SOUL

It began with the very sensitive matter of her pregnancy. Mary was betrothed to Joseph, and yet here she is with child. This appeared scandalous to anyone not privy to the truth. Jewish law gave Joseph the right to have her put to death, but being a just man, he sought to divorce her quietly. Even with this charitable act from her husband, Mary no doubt felt great pain at being incorrectly judged, and yet she remained silent.

Only when an angel of God comes to Joseph and tells him to take Mary as his wife, explaining the circumstances of the child she bore in her womb, do they join hands in marriage. But shortly after this, Caesar Augustus calls for his census, forcing the Holy Family to set out for Bethlehem just as Mary's due date approaches. Upon their arrival, they can find no room at the inn. There are no red carpets rolled out for the Mother of God, no parades, no celebrations, no comfort or honor.

Our Lord would be born in a stable, in a place where animals gathered. The nativity was a joyous moment for Mary and for Joseph, but still it was another example of the hardship Mary was forced to endure. Imagine the fear and worry for a woman traveling in the darkness, about to give birth, with nowhere to stay. Today, even with the comfort of modern medicine and technology and an endless amount of books, websites, and apps that walk us through the process of having a child, we grow sick with worry and concern. Who among us would not panic if we were in Mary and Joseph's shoes?

Things would get no easier for Mary when, according to Jewish custom, she and Joseph brought the Christ Child to present him at the Temple. Upon entering, they offer a sacrifice of two turtledoves, the sacrifice mandated by the Law of Moses for a poor family. It is then that the righteous and devout Simeon delivers his famous prophecy of the sword that would pierce her soul:

Behold, this child is set for the fall and rising of many in Israel,
and for a sign that is spoken against
(and a sword will pierce through your own soul also),
that thoughts out of many hearts may be revealed.

(Lk 2:34–35)

This was supposed to be a joyous occasion for Mary, yet here she is confronted by a prophecy of the suffering that awaits her. Though Mary knew she had a special child, she was not omniscient. She didn't know everything that would happen to her and to her son. Simeon's words would have come as a shock.

Yet she does not rebel at these words from God, so different from the joyful words delivered by the Archangel Gabriel less than a year earlier. She accepts these words too, painful as they are. She hears the word of God and accepts it.

Not much later, after the magi had come to adore the new King, Joseph again is visited by an angel who tells him to take his family and flee to Egypt in order to avoid the wrath of Herod. In contrast to the magi, Herod wanted to murder the new King, and in an attempt to do so, he ordered the killing of all male children in Bethlehem under the age of two.

The Holy Family was uprooted again, just as they were when they journeyed to Bethlehem for the census. Mary is still with child, only this time the infant is nestled in her arms and not in her womb. Another arduous journey is upon them as they flee to a land once hostile to their ancestors, with the threat of bloodthirsty soldiers seeking their child. This would have been a difficult trip, several weeks at least, across harsh and dangerous terrain.

Due to her sanctity, we can presume Mary cared more for the innocent children being slaughtered back in Bethlehem than the difficulties of her path. The Mother of the Church would go on to shed many tears throughout the centuries, tears over the suffering of her children, but these little souls, the first martyrs who died for her Son, were the first she would mourn with, the first who would cry with the Sorrowful Mother before entering their eternal reward.

THREE DAYS LOST

The Holy Family stayed in Egypt for several years until it was safe to return to Nazareth. Scripture gives us only one more account of Jesus's youth: He was twelve and traveled to Jerusalem for the feast of Passover with Mary and Joseph.

Passover in Jerusalem was a chaotic time when thousands of people flocked to the city in dozens of caravans. It would not be out of the ordinary for a boy to break away from his parents temporarily to travel with another group of pilgrims, among whom he might have cousins or friends.

A full day passed before Mary and Joseph realized Jesus was not with them or anyone they knew. We can imagine the panic they felt. If parents lose a child today for ten minutes at the mall or an amusement park, their bodies will nearly collapse from the trauma. But Mary was without Jesus for three days, searching for him with the tenacity of a grief-stricken mother.

Mary and Joseph would eventually find him in the Temple, speaking with the teachers and scholars of the law. This was obviously a moment of joy—indeed, it is one of the Joyful Mysteries of the Rosary—but the reunion between mother and child does not play out how we might expect. Mary approaches him and says,

"Son, why have you treated us so? Behold, your father and I have been looking for you anxiously." Jesus's response comes across as insensitive. "How is it that you sought me? Did you not know that I must be in my Father's house?" (Lk 2:48–49).

Jesus's words must have shocked Mary. She probably expected a hug, perhaps even an apology and a promise never to wander off again. But these acts of consolation that would have helped to mend her broken heart were withheld. It was a sign—a reminder—that her son was not ordinary, that his mission went far beyond his responsibilities as her child. Luke tells us she went back and pondered these things in her heart (see Lk 2:51).

After the finding in the Temple, Scripture leaps forward roughly two decades, leaving Mary and Jesus's hidden life in Nazareth to mystery. We are not shown their days and nights eating and praying together as a family. We do not see the morning hugs Mary and Jesus shared or the lessons Joseph gave Jesus in carpentry. We are not even shown the profound moment of Joseph's death. For whatever reason, God has chosen not to reveal these things to us.

The story picks back up years later when Jesus comes to be baptized in the Jordan River by his cousin, John the Baptist. Mary returns shortly after this at the wedding in Cana. She notes that the couple's wine has run dry and tells Jesus about this embarrassing situation. As with his response in the Temple as a boy, Jesus's reply comes across as curt: "O woman, what have you to do with me? My hour has not yet come" (Jn 2:4). Jesus goes on to turn the water to wine, but again his behavior toward his mother may give us pause. If he knew he was going to perform the miracle, why not respond with a more loving and receptive tone?

This would not be the last time Jesus, in his public ministry, obscured the love we know he had for Mary. In the eighth chapter of Luke, as Jesus preaches to a crowd, Mary and other family members approach but cannot get to him because of the press of people. Someone tells Jesus that his mother is trying to get to him.

When Mary presented the newborn Jesus in the Temple, Simeon told her a sword would pierce her soul. Her seven sorrows would begin to unfold at that very moment.

THE SORROWS OF MARY

The sorrows of Mary are a recurring subject of contemplation in the mystical tradition of the Church. Saints, blesseds, and religious who have recorded revelations about the sorrows of Mary include St. Elizabeth of Hungary (1207–1231), St. Bridget of Sweden (1303–1373), Blessed Veronica da Binasco (1445–1497), Venerable Maria of Ágreda (1602–1665), Blessed Anne Catherine Emmerich (1774–1824), Sister Josefa Menéndez (1890–1923), and Sister Lúcia of Fátima (1907–2005).

Oftentimes the revelations express a desire of the Lord to see Mary's sufferings commemorated by the faithful. In the *Glories of Mary,* St. Alphonsus Liguori recounts these words from Jesus to Blessed Veronica: *My daughter, tears shed for My Passion are dear to Me; but as I love My Mother Mary with an immense love, the meditation of the torments which she endured at My death is even more agreeable to Me.*

Another repeating feature of these private revelations is the promise of special graces to those who meditate on Mary's sorrows.

St. Elizabeth of Hungary said the Lord promised four special graces to those devoted to Mary's sufferings, including the following: *That those who before death invoke the Blessed Mother in the name of her sorrows, should obtain true repentance of all their sins.* And St. Bridget of Sweden, responsible for spreading the Seven Sorrows devotion, said Mary promised seven special graces to those who practice the devotion, including the following: *I will defend them in their spiritual battles with the infernal enemy and I will protect them at every instant of their lives.*

Instead of clearing a path, he says, "My mother and my brethren are those who hear the word of God and do it" (Lk 8:21). It's puzzling that he would not stop what he was doing to ensure Mary could get through to see him, and even more puzzling that he would say those who hear the word of God and do it are just as much his mother as she.

We see something similar in Luke, chapter 11, when a woman says, "Blessed is the womb that bore you, and the breasts that you sucked!" Jesus responds, "Blessed rather are those who hear the word of God and keep it!" (Lk 11:27–28). Here he is given a chance to bless Mary and preach to us about how wonderful she is, about how she will one day play a vital role in our salvation, about how she is the spiritual mother of every disciple, but he doesn't. Instead, he pivots away from her and delivers a different lesson about hearing the word of God and keeping it.

A TIME OF ABSENCE

These two instances in the Gospel of Luke puzzle Catholics and serve as fodder for those who would belittle Mary's role in God's plan. But the behavior Jesus shows toward his mother is not the only evidence for his apparent detachment from her. Her very absence during his public ministry speaks louder than any distance he might have displayed in her presence.

Where was Mary? Why was she not there for the parables and the miracles? Why, when crowds greeted him in a new town, was she not there too? If she would play such an important role in his Church, should she not have been more prevalent during his founding of it?

Mary surely would have loved to have been with Jesus when he cured the blind and healed the crippled or fed thousands by multiplying the loaves and fishes. Mothers are proud of their children when they eat their vegetables; imagine, then, how proud Mary would be if she witnessed Jesus doing all these things! And

LEFT
The Christ Child shows Mary instruments of his passion.

did she not deserve to be there? When the crowds laid down palms for him upon his arrival into Jerusalem, should she not also have been walking alongside him, as any queen does with her king?

But Mary is absent from these biblical scenes and does not return again until the darkest moment.

No words can describe the torment that afflicted her during her Son's passion and crucifixion. Losing a child is perhaps the worst pain a person can endure, and she not only witnessed his death, but his torture as well. She saw him scourged, mocked, and spat upon. She saw his clothes ripped off and a cross slung upon

ABOVE
Mary saw a cross slung upon Jesus's back, a cross he was forced to carry up a hill.

his back, a cross he was forced to carry up a hill and be crucified upon as he hung between two criminals. All his friends and followers abandoned him and his mother, except for John, the beloved disciple, and Mary Magdalene, the sinner.

We know that the story did not end there, that victory followed three days later. Christ is resurrected, and with his return, all humanity is offered eternal life. Yet nowhere in Scripture are we shown a reunion between mother and Son. We see him encounter his apostles and many others—hundreds laid eyes on the resurrected Christ—but if Mary was one of them, God has chosen not to tell us.

A review of these accounts from Scripture is necessary so we can grasp the full portrait of the Sorrowful Mother. Her suffering began long before the Crucifixion. Indeed, if we read Scripture attentively and attempt to experience events through the eyes of Mary, we can scarcely find a time when she is not suffering.

This is not to say her entire life was one of sorrow. Mary no doubt experienced great joy in those hidden years she spent with Jesus. So the question becomes not just why did Mary endure so much suffering but *why are we only shown the times of trial?* Why, when Mary appears in Scripture, do the pages always seem to be damp from her tears?

Like every facet of God's plan, there is a purpose to Mary's suffering, and a deeper reading of Sacred Scripture will help reveal this purpose.

Night of Faith

————— M —————

C H A P T E R

5

St. John of the Cross is the great teacher of the dark night of the soul. Though he did not officially coin the term, St. John wrote a poem in the sixteenth century that would eventually be given this name. The poem narrates the soul's journey to a deep, mystical union with God. This journey is called a dark night because the path is shrouded in darkness, as is the ultimate destination the soul is trying to reach—God. This darkness does not convey any sort of evil, but rather describes an unknowable mystery.

Since it is never pleasant to walk amidst darkness, the dark night, or night of faith, feels like a spiritual crisis. The dark night of the soul is a term that has come to describe a prolonged absence of light and hope, an extended melancholy over the apparent departure of God from one's life. Though the soul is progressing along a spiritual path that leads to its true home, the journey itself is agonizing. There are periods of profound and intense doubt as the soul falls into a kind of spiritual depression.

St. Paul of the Cross is said to have suffered from his dark night for almost fifty years. St. Thérèse of Lisieux, the Little Flower, suffered from a deep spiritual darkness as well. St. Teresa of Calcutta may be the most well-known case of the dark night. She once wrote in a letter to her spiritual director, "In my soul, I feel that terrible pain of loss, of God not wanting me, of God not being God, of God not existing."

How are we to make sense of such a strange occurrence: that a woman so revered for her holiness would feel the agony of losing God? And what purpose could God have in detaching himself from us in such a way?

In the dark night, God teaches us to love him for his own sake and not for the blessings he bestows upon us. It's easy to love God on Christmas morning as you sit with your children and tally your blessings amidst a warm cocoon of love and joy. To love God as you hang on a cross is quite another feat. An intense detachment, not only from sin, but even from created things good in themselves, even from spiritual consolations, is the only way to bring about such a radical and mystical union.

Fulton Sheen, in *The World's First Love,* remarked that Christ "begins detaching himself from his mother, seemingly alienating his affections with growing unconcern—only to reveal at the very end that what he was doing was introducing her through sorrow to a new and deeper dimension of love."[3]

St. John Paul II said something similar. In *Redemptoris Mater,* he commented on the sorrows Our Lady bore throughout her life and identified them as a "night of faith . . . through which one has to draw near to the Invisible One and to live in intimacy with the mystery."

SORROW AND UNION

The first glimpse we get of Mary's sorrow comes shortly after her return from Judea, where she spent several months with Elizabeth. Upon her return, she is nearly divorced by Joseph, who does not yet understand her pregnancy.

One might expect Mary to defend herself. But she does not. Fr. Philippe speaks beautifully to the purpose and faith behind Mary's silence:

---

[3] Venerable Fulton J. Sheen, *The World's First Love* (San Francisco: Ignatius Press, 2015), p. 84.

> We should take note of Mary's silence in the mystery of the Annunciation, which is the sign of her contemplative life and a safeguard for her divine solitude. This silence is the direct consequence of the secret covenant that exists between her and God. . . . It is not at all a violent and forced silence, like Zechariah's silence (a punitive silence, a quarantine); it is a free and loving silence. . . . This silence . . . isolates Mary from Joseph. In this respect, *it implies a certain divine trial for Mary. . . . It is a divine means which intensifies the life of union with God and which at the same time separates one from all human community, however holy it may be.*[4]

Mary shows incredible faith in not defending her honor. She puts everything in God's hands and trusts that he will take care of her, and this is precisely what he does when he sends an angel to Joseph. The angel says, "Joseph, son of David, do not fear to take Mary your wife, for that which is conceived in her is of the Holy Spirit; she will bear a son, and you shall call his name Jesus, for he will save his people from their sins" (Mt 1:20–21). Being a man of faith, Joseph obeyed and "did as the angel of the Lord commanded him" (Mt 1:24).

It would not have been shameful for Mary to defend herself. It would not have been a sin to defend her purity. But in her silence, she shows her faith in God. She is denying herself for a greater good.

The trials of her pregnancy do not end once the angel enlightens Joseph. Within a few months, she will undertake the journey to Bethlehem and be forced to have her child in a stable, an abandoned cave where animals gathered.

Yet this was exactly what Divine Providence ordered, and for a most important reason. Our Lord came into the world to tell us that the first shall be last (see Mt 20:16), and so his arrival came

---

[4] Fr. Marie-Dominique Philippe, OP, *The Mysteries of Mary: Growing in Faith, Hope, and Love with the Mother of God* (Charlotte, NC: TAN Books, 2011), pp. 93-94; emphasis added.

where the last would gather, hidden in the darkness in the recesses of the earth. He came to save sinners, to heal the sick, to preach the good news to the poor, and to live a common life hidden from his people for thirty years. He did not come to entertain kings and be served in palace dining halls.

Christ came into the world precisely how he intended to, a way that mirrors how we often find him in our own lives. We find Jesus in silence, not in the hustle and bustle of everyday life. This is where Mary needed to see him first as well, in the solitude of that cave. The mystery had to be hidden for it to take root in her heart. The intimacy of Our Lord's arrival is reserved for Mary, as Joseph stands by protecting the moment, so that she can begin to form that mystical bond.

The Lord knew Mary was not destined for the life of an earthly queen, nor would her humility allow it. It would not have been fitting for her to be welcomed with pomp and ceremony, knowing the path that lay before her and her son. The rejection of Mary and the infant Jesus in Bethlehem was a foreshadowing of the rejection he would face thirty-three years later. Providence led her to the lowest place on earth to bear her Son, knowing he

ABOVE
"Rise, take the child and his mother, and flee to Egypt" (Mt 2:13).

would redeem the world by starting at the bottom and ascending the hill of Calvary. He began his earthly life in a cave in the sweet embrace of her arms and ended it in her arms after he was taken down from the Cross.

Shortly after his birth, the devout Simeon warns Mary of the sword that would pierce her soul. Here at the presentation of Jesus, Mary begins to understand that her own fate is bound up with the fate of her Son. Just as the lance would pierce his side on the Cross, her soul would be pierced by a spiritual sword. His agony was visible and bloody; hers, invisible and spiritual, but both were part of God's plan. His suffering and sacrifice would redeem humanity; hers would make her Mother of the Church.

Next, consider the Holy Family's flight into Egypt. This could be seen as the devil's first attack since the birth of Jesus.

ABOVE
Just as the lance would pierce Jesus's side on the Cross, Mary's soul would be pierced by a spiritual sword.

The Annunciation and Nativity took place in anonymity, beyond his watchful gaze, but finally he senses something new in the air. He works through Herod to order the slaughter of the innocents, searching for this new King in order to murder him. Again, Mary is stricken by sorrow as well as fear and terror.

But this occasion of sorrow helps form her obedience and faith. Remember that the angel came to Joseph and warned *him* to flee. Thus, Mary must submit to his role as the head of the family. Her obedience to Joseph helps form her obedience to God, and she trusts in them both as they journey into the night to a distant land without even knowing how long they will be gone.

This is not an act of cowardice, of fleeing from the battle against evil. It is, rather, a strategic retreat to prepare for the time when the battle will be most acutely upon them.

In this period of exile, Mary is again hidden and alone with her Son. His first years are spent away from their people, intensifying her union with him once again. Just as sorrow in our own lives causes us to withdraw from everyday life and seek comfort in Christ, she too finds an occasion of fear and sorrow to be an opportunity to deepen her bond with him. A pattern is developing as *the sorrow fortifies the union.*

A TIME OF PREPARATION

A kind of turning point of the mother and Son's relationship comes years later, after Jesus is lost for three days and eventually found in the Temple. In past moments of difficulty, she at least still remained in his presence, but now she is separated from him. It's easy for us to question why Jesus would do this to his mother, why he would wander off like this, or at least not warn her that he would be gone for a number of days. But he could not warn her because the anguish in her heart had to be felt with full intensity. Only then could he prepare her for the next time she would be without him for three days.

Photograph of St. Thérèse of Lisieux (1873-97), c. 1895. St. Thérèse endured a profound night of faith, which she compared to being enveloped in dark mists that "sink deep into my soul and wrap it round."

ST. THÉRÈSE AND THE DARK NIGHT

St. Thérèse of Lisieux is known and loved throughout the world for her "Little Way"—a path to holiness characterized not by great deeds, grand renunciations, and fearsome penances but by daily acts of love and confidence in God.

Yet for all her littleness, St. Thérèse's own holiness was forged in a great trial, that of the dark night of the soul. Her autobiography, *Story of a Soul,* recounts her loss of the joy of faith. Suffering from tuberculosis, aware that her death was likely months away, she wrote that the veil of faith "is no longer a veil for me, it is a wall" and that she had no consolation in the thought of heaven. Yet her darkness, instead of quenching, increased her faith and inspired in her a desire to suffer for the conversion of unbelievers and the love of God.

> Ah! may Jesus pardon me if I have caused Him any pain, but He knows very well that while I do not have the joy of faith, I am trying to carry out its works at least. . . . I tell Him I am ready to shed my blood to the last drop to profess my faith in the existence of heaven. I tell Him, too, I am happy not to enjoy this beautiful heaven on this earth so that He will open it for all eternity to poor unbelievers. . . . [I]s there a joy greater than that of suffering out of love for You? The more interior the suffering is and the less apparent to the eyes of creatures, the more it rejoices You, O my God!

The time and circumstance of this event cannot be over-looked. It was the feast of Passover and they were in Jerusalem. Roughly two decades later, he would journey within the walls of Jerusalem and be crucified, ripping him away from her for three days again. Her agony here prepared her for that moment.

But Christ's absence was not the only preparation he sought to give his mother; his reaction to being found also bore a prepa-ratory purpose. Instead of apologizing for the worry he caused, or promising to never wander off again, he replies, "How is it that you sought me? Did you not know that I must be in my Father's house?" Luke tells us that Mary and Joseph "did not understand the saying which he spoke to them" (2:49–50). Mary is confused by Jesus's words, and we can sympathize with her confusion. This is not the response we would expect from a loving and well-behaved child.

Jesus was, as it seemed on the surface, beginning to detach himself from her in order to draw her into a mystical union with him. He couldn't give her that human interaction when she found him, that consolation she yearned for. Such a reaction would have tethered her to the role of his earthly mother, and he had bigger plans for her.

The next eighteen years pass under the cloak of anonymity. God did not choose to disclose these hidden years of Jesus and Mary's life except to say that he was obedient to Joseph and Mary and that he "increased in wisdom and in stature, and in favor with God and man" (Lk 2:51–52).

Why the hidden life? We do not know, but we know God has a purpose in all things. Surely Jesus could have begun his min-istry earlier than he did, perhaps even right then in the Temple when she found him, for the scholars of the law were amazed by his wisdom (see Lk 2:47). But the fact remains that he waited many years.

Perhaps he was preparing his mother to assume her future role as Mother of the Church. Or perhaps God willed that Jesus

LEFT
Jesus detached himself from Mary in order to draw her into a mystical union.

73

spend this hidden time with his mother to better prepare him for what awaited.

Whatever the reason, the story of Mary picks back up at the wedding at Cana, when she implores her son to turn his attention to the poor couple's embarrassing situation. Yet he answers, "O woman, what have you to do with me? My hour has not yet come" (Jn 2:4).

It might surprise us that he would address her as "woman," since it comes across as aloof and cold. And he would do this again later as he hung on the Cross. Yet there was a purpose behind his words. Both these instances harken back to the language used in the Garden when God promised that a woman would come and be placed in enmity to the serpent. Jesus is pointing to the *protoevangelium,* showing his mother her place in God's plan.

Still more, the two times Jesus calls her "woman" are linked in another way. When Jesus asks, "What have you to do with me? My hour has not yet come," he is asking, "What, Mary, do you have to do with my hour? With my passion and crucifixion?" This is what his "hour" is referring to.

We should be clear that Jesus never asks a question to receive an answer—he already knows everything—so when he does, he is inviting that person, as well as all of us, to think about something in a deeper way. Jesus is asking what the lack of wine has to do with Mary and his passion.

The answer is that Mary is inextricably linked to that hour, the hour when the serpent will be crushed, just as she is linked to its prefiguring at Cana. What seems like a rebuke of his mother is actually a way for Jesus to show the intercessory role Mary plays. He is communicating that just as he would not perform the miracle of turning water into wine without her, so too he will not redeem us without her. This moment was the catalyst for his ministry and what made his disciples begin to believe in him (see Jn 2:11).

Finally, let us address those two passages in the Gospel of Luke where Jesus does not get up to greet his mother and does not

No words can des-
cribe the torment that
afflicted Mary during
her Son's passion
and crucifixion.

ABOVE
Mary was Jesus's
first disciple and
shares in his glory.

take the chance to bless her when given the opportunity. We can presume this lack of affection might have hurt Mary, or at least confused her. In both those instances, Jesus seems to deflect her importance, instead stressing the importance of those who "hear the word of God and keep it." But, in fact, this is simply a veiled way of praising Mary.

"Is not Mary the first of 'those who hear the word of God and do it,'" asks St. John Paul II in *Redemptoris Mater*. "And therefore does not the blessing uttered by Jesus in response to the woman in the crowd refer primarily to her?" Mary is not only the mother of Jesus. She is the first disciple, the preeminent disciple, the most faithful steward of God's grace. That is why of all creatures she has been given the highest throne.

A CROWN OF GLORY

All that Mary was put through, from the prophecy of Simeon, to the flight into Egypt, to the loss of Jesus in the Temple, to the confusion of her son's behavior at times, was simply a preparation for the Cross.

After watching him be scourged, mocked, and spat upon, after watching him carry the cross that he would be nailed to, Mary stands at her Son's feet. She is there to the bloody end. Her presence both comforts Jesus *and* makes his pain more acute, for he hates to see her in such agony. He no doubt wishes she would *not* have to be there, to keep her from witnessing his agonizing death. But she is there. She has to be, for this is when he must hand her over to us, when she must become our mother. He looks down and sees her standing beside the beloved disciple, John, and to Mary he says, "Woman, behold, your son!" And to John, "Behold, your mother!" (Jn 19:26–27).

We must understand that Jesus was not establishing a mother-son bond solely with John, but with all of us. Note that Scripture does not address John by name, but rather says, "then he said to *the disciple.*" We are all called to be disciples of Christ, and so we can all stand at the foot of his cross alongside his suffering mother. Scripture says John took Mary into his own home from that hour on. As her other sons and daughters, we are called to do the same, to take her into our hearts.

We might ask why Jesus chose this moment to hand Mary over to us as our mother. Why not at some point earlier in his ministry, perhaps at the Last Supper? Why not at a moment of peace when it wouldn't be overshadowed by the drama of the Crucifixion? What is the significance of the timing here?

It seems there are likely several reasons. The moment is perhaps most significant because it comes when Jesus has nothing left to give us. For three years, he has healed and taught and forgiven sins, but in his dying breath, as he gives the ultimate sacrifice of himself, he also gives us his most precious creation.

This is also the time for Jesus to give Mary to us because she is now ready. Everything she endured prepared her for this moment. The detachment Jesus displayed toward her and her many sorrows formed her so that here, at the height of her sorrow, she could deny one good for a greater good.

She could participate in the sacrifice of her son, offer her fiat once again, not to the incarnation of her Son, but to his death. This was the moment she became the mother of humanity, and the agony she felt at the foot of the Cross was her childbearing pain. Fr. Philippe speaks beautifully of this moment when she let go of Jesus and embraced us all: "While her mother's heart really must consent to die at the foot of the Cross, her heart as the new Eve, in contrast, begins to beat."[5]

Note Jesus's use of the word *woman* again. He is harkening back to the last time he called her this, when she prompted him to change the water to wine. Now he is giving us not wine but his own blood, the eternal wine. He is also harkening back to the Garden, to the woman who would be placed in enmity with the serpent. But it was not just enmity between her and the serpent, but between her seed and his. Now that she has become the mother of humanity, it is not just Jesus who is her seed, but all of us—the Body. Thus, the children of Mary and the children of Satan will also be at odds with one another, and we will see this playing out for the next two millennia.

After Jesus expires, a Roman soldier pierces his side with a lance to ensure he is truly dead. This last act is reserved solely for Mary's own anguish. Jesus is already dead; he feels no pain from this. But from where she stands just a few feet away, Mary feels the sword piercing her soul—the one Simeon spoke of. Blood and water pour from Jesus's side, a symbol of the sacramental grace we receive through his Church in Baptism and the Eucharist. As Eve was pulled from Adam's side, the Church, his bride, is here pulled from the side of Christ. And this most powerful moment is

---

[5] Ibid., p. 251.

wrapped up in Mary's agony, she who would become the Mother of the Church.

At the foot of the Cross, Mary's dark night is nearly complete. She still must witness her Son's mutilated body being taken down from the Cross and placed in the tomb, the last of her seven sorrows according to the Sorrowful Mother devotion. He is covered in spices, wrapped in linen, and placed in a sepulcher. Just as he was born in a cave, rejected by humanity, he is returned to a cave in the same manner.

These three days that pass after his death mirror the three when she lost him as a boy. Unlike then, when she actively sought him, here she knows she cannot engage in any such search. She will not find him as she did in the Temple. Thus, the pain is amplified when the stone is rolled over the mouth of the cave.

But she is not without hope, because she is not without faith. We don't know if Mary understood that Jesus would rise three days later. It is possible she heard of his claims to rebuild the Temple in three days. Would she have understood what this meant? Clearly, the apostles did not. Yet Mary was different from them in so many ways.

Scripture does not give us any evidence of a reunion between Mary and Jesus after the Resurrection. Instead, it gives us accounts of Jesus appearing to those who did not have the faith she did.

The first to see the resurrected Christ, Mary Magdalene, thought the authorities had stolen Jesus's body; when he appeared to her, she did not recognize him but supposed he was a gardener (see Jn 20:15). When she told the others she had seen him, they did not believe her; the disciples thought she was telling an "idle tale" (Lk 24:11) for which they are later rebuked by Jesus (see Mk 16:11–14).

Consider, too, the disciples on the road to Emmaus, who did not know it was Jesus walking alongside them. Jesus would say to them, "O foolish men, and slow of heart to believe all that the prophets have spoken!" (Lk 24:25). And of course there is doubting Thomas, who refuses to believe in the resurrected Lord until he places his fingers in the holy wounds of Christ (see Jn 20:24–29).

Would Mary have suffered from any of this confusion and doubt? Would she have looked upon him, her Son, and supposed he was a gardener? Would she not have recognized him on that road to Emmaus? If someone told her he had risen, would she refuse to believe and demand to place her fingers into his sides? Surely not!

Perhaps Scripture only shows us those who lacked perfect faith because in them we see ourselves. We can read in *The Glories of Mary* that St. Albert the Great once said, "Mary exercised perfect faith. For even when the disciples were doubting, she did not doubt." If we were honest, we would know we are much more like the doubting apostles than the faithful virgin.

Or perhaps we are not shown a reunion between Mary and Jesus after the Resurrection because, as some have speculated, we are not worthy to witness it. Mary and Jesus had shared, and would share, themselves with all humanity. But perhaps they wanted to keep the mystery of their love and union in this moment for themselves.

Most scholars say it would be fitting for Jesus to return to his mother, and therefore we can presume he did. St. Ignatius makes reference to this possible meeting in his *Spiritual Exercises,* saying that Jesus would have appeared to Mary first to assure her he was okay. But others might argue that, because of her perfect faith, she needed no visible sign of the Resurrection, that she is the one who Christ speaks of preeminently when addressing the doubt of Thomas: "Blessed are those who have not seen and yet believe" (Jn 20:29).

Whether she saw him or not, we do not know. But we do know she had perfect faith in her Son. Even if she did not fully understand the particulars of his plan, she knew by faith he would fulfill his promise to redeem humanity. This trust she had in him, though, in no way lessened the grief she felt at his violent

departure from this world. When our loved ones die, we grieve and sorrow over their absence from us—even if we have good reason to hope the Lord will grant them "a place of refreshment, light and peace."

And so it was for Mary. She was a grief-stricken mother who had lost and buried her Son. Yet she was also his first disciple who, because of the long and sorrowful path she had traversed, was prepared to receive her crown of glory.

ABOVE
Mary believed Jesus would fulfill his promise to redeem humanity.

All Generations Will Call Me Blessed

CHAPTER

6

In the Gospel of Luke, Mary says in her *Magnificat,* "For behold, henceforth all generations will call me blessed" (Lk 1:48). How wonderfully accurate these words have been.

Across the generations the Church came to see more and more the role of Mary in God's plan. The Church defined the four Marian dogmas: her divine motherhood, her perpetual virginity, her immaculate conception, and her assumption into heaven. The faithful, meanwhile, adopted the great Marian devotions: litanies, scapulars, the Rosary, the Miraculous Medal, Marian consecration, and many more.

These devotions were—and are—ways of both praising Mary and invoking her protection. For despite the devil's crushing defeat at Calvary, his battle for souls continued. In the struggle against him, the faithful would come to learn what a powerful advocate they had in their Queen.

MOTHER OF THE CHURCH

The relative anonymity of Our Lady's life in Scripture robs us of a narrative we long to know: What happened to Mary in the last part of her life, after the passion of Our Lord?

The Bible is not completely silent. The Acts of the Apostles tells us that Mary was with the apostles at Pentecost. She remained with them in the upper room for nine days of prayer, giving birth to our tradition of the novena. Mary, as Mother of the Church, is present at the birth of the Church, praying with and for the apostles as they prepared to take the gospel to the nations.

But the Bible *is* silent on where Mary went from here. The whereabouts of Mary's last years is debated; some say she was in Jerusalem, while others say the Apostle John, charged by the Lord to care for her, brought her to Ephesus in modern day Turkey. In the nineteenth century, a little stone house was discovered on a hillside in Ephesus where it is believed Mary lived.

The house was discovered mainly through the visions of the mystic Blessed Ann Catherine Emmerich who gave remarkable and specific details about the house and the area around it, including the rocky hillside that rose out of the Aegean Sea and even an old castle that sat miles away. Sister Emmerich claimed that this was where Mary spent her last years and was assumed into heaven. This house in Ephesus came to be called *Panaya Kapulu*, meaning "Doorway to the Virgin," and several popes have gone there to visit and celebrate Mass. Oddly enough, it has become a place where both Christians and Muslims come to pray in peace.

One of the most interesting things about this story of Mary going to Ephesus is the theory that she was the first to walk the Stations of the Cross. Blessed Anne Catherine said that when John brought her to this mountain, she laid out a path for the Stations, the distance of which corresponded to Christ's ascent to Calvary, and that she walked and prayed these Stations every day. When the house in Ephesus was discovered, gatherings of rocks were found in circles, spaced out evenly in a pattern behind the home. They had Jewish engravings on them; the markings were translated to be markers for the Stations of the Cross. There's no way to know for certain about any of this, but it helps vivify our imagination and form visuals of Mary's last years.

The Church has never ruled on the exact location of Mary's last moments on earth, but wherever she was, her life would not conclude like all other creatures. At the end of her earthly life, Our Lord would intervene in a miraculous way and assume his mother into heaven. The assumption of Mary was declared a dogma of the Catholic Church in 1950. Yet the belief had been held since apostolic times. We see evidence for this in the absence of any tradition of her relics.

From the very beginning, the Church prized the bodily relics of her saints. The bones of those martyred in the Colosseum, for instance, were quickly gathered up and preserved, as were the bones of St. Peter and St. Paul in Rome. If Mary was treated differently, it is because she left no bones to preserve, no bodily relics or remains.

In 1950, when Pius XII defined the dogma of the Assumption, he left open the question of whether Mary passed through death before being assumed or simply fell asleep, as in the Eastern tradition of the Dormition. What is defined is that Mary, "having completed the course of her earthly life, was assumed body and soul into heavenly glory."

Pius IX defined the dogma of the Immaculate Conception in 1854.

THE MARIAN DOGMAS

Mary's assumption showed the apostles and the first generation of Christians her special place in God's plan. It was one of the first glories of God's masterpiece to be revealed. But subsequent generations would discover more and more of her glories, including discerning her title of *Theotókos,* "Mother of God."

The dogma dates to the Council of Ephesus in 431. About 250 bishops, led by St. Cyril of Alexandria, had been convened by Emperor Theodosius II to address the archbishop of Constantinople, Nestorius. Nestorius had refused to allow the traditional practice of calling Mary "Mother of God." He argued that Mary could not be the mother of Jesus's divinity, but only of his humanity. In response, the Council condemned him and affirmed that Mary is *Mater Dei* ("the Mother of God") or *Theotókos* ("the God-bearer"). They reasoned that if the man Jesus is God and if Mary is his mother, she is rightly then the Mother of God.

Mary's divine motherhood was the first Marian dogma defined by the Church. It is first, not only in time, but also in theological priority: It is precisely because Mary is the mother of God that she is, in the words of *Lumen Gentium,* "enriched by God with the gifts which befit such a role" (LG 56).

One of these gifts is Mary's immaculate conception. This dogma states that Mary was conceived without sin in the womb of her mother through the foreseen merits of her Son. Pius IX defined the dogma in 1854, but it was believed and celebrated long before that. Sixtus IV established the feast of the Immaculate Conception in 1476, and there's evidence of it being celebrated back into the fifth century.

Indeed, the first to recognize Mary's immaculate conception was the Archangel Gabriel, when he hailed her at the Annunciation as "full of grace"—that is, without even the least stain of sin.

The Mother of God was also a virgin—before, during, and after the birth of her Son. Her perpetual virginity was yet another

gift from God. It was a gift that empowered her to live out her role in God's plan of salvation and to be available to Jesus and to us all. It freed her to "follow the Lamb wherever he goes," as it says of the virgins in the Book of Revelation.

We're given a clue about Mary's virginity in the Gospel of Luke. It says she was betrothed to Joseph, and yet when she's told she would have a son, she asks, "How can this be?" (Lk 1:34). It's a strange question for a betrothed woman to ask, unless she's taken a vow of virginity.

The dogma of Mary's perpetual virginity reminds us that it was not the will of man that brought Jesus into the world, but the will of God. As First Corinthians tells us, the first man was from the earth, a man of dust, but the new man was from heaven (see 1 Cor 15:47). If he was from heaven, then he came not from a man; and if he came not from a man, then his mother was truly a virgin.

The *Catechism* is clear about the virgin birth. Mary was a virgin before, during, and after the birth of Christ. The *Catechism* points out that Christ's birth did not diminish his mother's virginal integrity, but sanctified it.

People are sometimes taken aback to see references to the brothers of Jesus in the Bible. But Jesus did not have any siblings. The Church has always understood those passages as referring to close relations. There are no words in Hebrew or Aramaic for cousin, uncle, or nephew; *brother* is used for them all. Lot and Abraham, for example, call each other brother in Genesis, though Lot was actually Abraham's nephew. And St. Matthew specifies that James and Joseph, whom he calls brothers of Jesus, were actually the sons of another Mary, a disciple of Christ (see Mt 27:56).

Mary remained a virgin all her life. This, says the *Catechism*, was a sign of her faith, of her undivided gift of herself to God.

MARIAN DEVOTIONS

These are the dogmas of our Faith concerning Mary: her divine motherhood, her perpetual virginity, her immaculate conception, and her assumption into heaven. These are the four pillars of belief the Church has given us regarding Mary. They form the very foundation of Marian spirituality and support the many prayers, devotions, and spiritual practices that can draw us ever closer to the *Theotókos*—God's mother and ours.

But to understand Our Lady's role in the Church we mustn't look only to the dogmas and creeds. Across the generations, we have come to call Mary blessed not just because of Church councils

The Rosary is a weapon for spiritual warfare. Its power was first
demonstrated after Mary recommended it to St. Dominic (ABOVE)
as a means to convert the Albigensians.

THE ROSARY AND ALBEGENSIANISM

In the year 1208, the Albigensian heresy was flourishing in southern France. A neo-Manichean movement that denied the Incarnation and despised the flesh, Albigensianism forbade its adherents from marrying and having children and encouraged suicide by starvation.

St. Dominic, founder of the order that bears his name, launched a campaign to convert the Albigensians through his preaching. But he met with little success. Defeated, he withdrew to the forest to pray and fast and beg God for assistance.

Three days later, he was visited by the Queen of Heaven. *Dear Dominic, do you know which weapon the Blessed Trinity wants to use to reform the world?* Mary asked.

When Dominic responded that he did not, Mary told him, *I want you to know that, in this kind of warfare, the battering ram has always been the Angelic Psalter which is the foundation stone of the New Testament. Therefore if you want to reach these hardened souls and win them over to God, preach my Psalter.*

By "Angelic Psalter," Mary was recommending to Dominic the recitation of the Hail Mary (the "Angelic Salutation") 150 times (the length of the Psalter).

St. Dominic did as Mary asked, grouping the prayers into the Joyful, Sorrowful, and Glorious mysteries to form the Rosary. As he began preaching the Rosary to the Albigensians, he inspired many conversions.

In 1213, the Catholic commander Simon de Montfort fought a decisive battle against the Albigensian forces in the town of Muret. De Montfort's forces were in the habit of praying the Rosary at the suggestion of St. Dominic. They won a victory at Muret that they deemed miraculous. De Montfort built the first chapel in honor of the Rosary there in gratitude.

and declarations that defined who she was but because she has lived on with us in the life of the Church, providing both protection from adversaries and maternal care and love.

The first indications of Marian veneration could be seen as early as the end of the first century when Mary was depicted in frescos in the Roman catacombs, both with and without her Son. There is a fresco in the catacombs of St. Agnes that shows her standing between St. Peter and St. Paul, extending her hands out to them. These men were symbols of Christ's Church, so in this fresco, we see a symbol of Mary as Mother of the Church. Mary's prominent position between St. Peter and St. Paul shows the love and esteem of the early Church for the mother of the Lord.

The most ancient prayer to the Blessed Mother, called the *Sub Tuum Praesidium*, dates back to the year 250:

> *We fly to your patronage,*
> *O holy Mother of God,*
> *despise not our petitions*
> *in our necessities,*
> *but deliver us from all dangers.*
> *O ever glorious and blessed Virgin.*

In addition to the ancient art and prayers would come cathedrals and feasts dedicated to Mary, and countless girls would be named in her honor. Millions of women would seek to imitate Mary's humility, chastity, and charity by entering consecrated life, transforming the Church and the world with their prayers and good works. More broadly, historians have noted that devotion to Mary prompted a change in how women were viewed in society, spurring the development of chivalry and achieving for women a dignified respect that had never before been given.

The wealth of art, music, and architecture dedicated to Mary vivifies our love for her. But we mustn't forget that they are only reminders that she is really and truly with us still. Death did not claim her. She is not in the grave, but rather body and soul in

LEFT
Mary provides both protection from adversaries and maternal care to the Church.

heaven. And from there she can come, and at times *has* come, in striking ways. She has come to watch over us and to intercede for us in the darkest moments of our history, when the evil one was poised to attack.

Consider the great Marian devotions. Almost all of them came from her own hands. The Miraculous Medal, for example, stems from apparitions of Our Lady to St. Catherine Labouré. In the thirteenth century, she gave St. Simon Stock the Brown Scapular, promising that anyone who dies wearing it will be saved. And of course the most famous gift Mary has given us is the Rosary.

The tradition of the Rosary goes back centuries in the Church. The earliest monks prayed all 150 psalms daily and would use beads or pebbles to track their prayers. Many lay people desired to imitate them but, being unable to read, could not pray the psalms. They substituted *Hail Mary's* instead, thus giving rise to the Rosary. But the devotion would develop and spread only after Mary appeared to St. Dominic in 1214, telling him that the Rosary was *the weapon the Blessed Trinity wants to use to reform the world.*

At key moments in history, the faithful have always sought the intercession of Mary. Perhaps at none of these moments were the stakes higher than during the Battle of Lepanto in 1571, when the Ottoman Empire was expanding into eastern Europe and ravaging everything in its path. Constantinople had fallen to Islam over one hundred years earlier, leaving the Balkans and Hungary open to conquest. With the Turks raiding the coast of Italy, the control of the Mediterranean was at stake. It was in this desperate time that the Holy Father turned to Mary.

Pope Pius V organized a fleet under the command of Don Juan of Austria. While preparations were underway, the Holy Father, an ardent follower of St. Dominic, asked all the faithful to say the Rosary and implore our Blessed Mother's prayers, asking that the Lord grant victory to the Christian fleet.

Don Juan's forces went into battle against the Ottomans on October 7, 1571 at Lepanto and defeated an empire despite being

Mary is the Mother of the Church, praying with and for the apostles as they take the gospel to all nations.

drastically outnumbered. It was truly a miracle. Pius instituted a new feast—Our Lady of the Holy Rosary—in honor of her inter-cession that day. It's no exaggeration to say the world as we know it would be far different had it not been for the victory at Lepanto.

At so many times in history, when heresy festered and evil threatened, Our Lady has come and protected us with her loving embrace. As we will see, the one who was assumed into heaven has come down and appeared to us, not randomly or without reason, but precisely when her children were most in danger and the assaults of the evil one had reached a critical point.

Such a critical level would be reached in the sixteenth century in the Aztec Empire of the New World, where human sacrifice and pagan worship gripped the land. Here, Mary would, in dramatic fashion, liberate a people from demonic practices and usher in the largest mass conversion in the history of the Church.

LEFT
The most famous
devotion Mary
has given us is
the Rosary.

Mother of the Americas

CHAPTER

7

One of the most striking of Christ's statements

is his promise that the gates of hell will not prevail against the Church.

This rather mysterious phrase can be interpreted in various ways. It is most often understood in a defensive sense: When enemies and error threaten the Church, like barbarians besieging a city, the Lord will protect her and defend her from fatal assaults.

But Christ's words may also be understood in an *offensive* way. As the prince of this world, Satan has his own cities and strongholds. But these strongholds are no match for the Church. Christ has given his disciples power to smash their gates, conquer their wicked rulers, and bring the gospel to the inhabitants within.

One of Satan's strongholds was the Aztec Empire, where human sacrifice was practiced on an industrial scale. The atrocities of the Aztecs rivaled those of Canaan and Carthage from before the time of Christ. They were a people trapped behind the gates of hell.

But five hundred years ago, those gates were smashed, their rulers overthrown, and a Woman stronger than their pagan gods would come to them as their mother. She would come to set them free.

THE HORNS OF SATAN

The dark rituals that dominated Aztec life can be hard to fathom.

Most Aztec towns were built around pyramid-like temples. On the top of these pyramids, black-robed Aztec priests would kill slaves, prisoners, virgins, and babies. They would hold them down on a rock by their arms and legs. Then the Aztec priest would cut out their hearts while the victims were still alive and hold them up in front of the people as a sacrifice to the gods.

ABOVE
The conquistador Hernán Cortés wrote that the Aztec practice of human sacrifice "is the most terrible and frightful thing" his men ever witnessed.

The great G. K. Chesterton speaks in *The Everlasting Man* of the Aztec culture being a place where "the horns of Satan were exalted . . . in the face of the sun." Only a culture in thrall to demons would revel in such gruesomeness and exalt such bloody human sacrifice. Chesterton argued that the Aztecs were working backwards against their own nature not just by celebrating the killing of their own people but by depicting their gods in hideous and grotesque forms. Compare this to the Greeks, who worshipped pagan gods, but at least viewed them as graceful and beautiful. The Greeks did not have the benefit of divine revelation but were still in accord with humanity's natural inclination to appreciate beauty. The Aztecs, under the control of demonic forces, were rebelling against this natural appreciation of beauty.[6]

After the Spanish forces conquered the Aztecs, missionaries arrived on the wild shores of Mexico. They erected Catholic churches where pagan gods once reigned and built schools and hospitals. Slowly, they attempted to transform the ancient Aztec culture into a Christian one.

But the pagan practices were hard to uproot and conversions to Christianity were few. The missionary bishop Juan de Zumarraga wrote to the king of Spain that, if heaven did not intervene, the land was all but lost. Bishop Zumarraga implored the help of Our Lady, asking her to send him Castilian roses, then unknown in Mexico, as a sign that she had heard his plea.

A MOTHER COMES

On a chilly morning in 1531, a poor peasant named Juan Diego wrapped his *tilma*, or cloak, tightly around his shoulders and set out on the long walk to attend Mass. It was the feast of the Immaculate Conception, then celebrated on December 9.

Six years earlier, Juan Diego, his wife, Maria, and his uncle Juan Bernardino had been baptized. They were among the small number of Aztecs to be received into the Church. Juan Diego

---

[6] G. K. Chesteron, *The Everlasting Man* (New York: Image Books, 1955), pp. 122-124.

loved his Catholic faith. But then Maria died, childless, and Juan suffered from intense loneliness.

As he journeyed to the church, Juan Diego approached a hill known as Tepeyac, where there had once been a shrine to the pagan mother goddess Tonantzin. He was surprised to hear beautiful music filling the morning air; its power overwhelmed him as it poured down from heaven.

ABOVE
Only a culture in thrall to demons would exalt such bloody human sacrifice.

103

He then saw a glowing cloud, lit up by the dazzling lights of a rainbow. When the music stopped, a delicate voice called out his name. He followed the voice, climbing over boulders toward the summit of the hill, and found himself face-to-face with a Lady.

She told Juan Diego that she was the Virgin Mary, Mother of the True God. And she said she wanted a new shrine built here where she could show her love and compassion for the people.

Juan Diego went at once to the bishop, telling him of Mary's request. But Bishop Zumarraga was skeptical and sent Juan Diego away.

ABOVE
A miraculous spring gushed forth on Mary's third visit to Juan Diego.

Juan Diego was devastated. He came back to Tepeyac and begged Our Lady to choose a more prominent messenger, one the bishop would not be so ready to dismiss. Our Lady just smiled at him. *I have chosen you,* she said.

Again, Juan Diego approached the bishop, and again he was met with skepticism. The bishop grilled him, searching for any reason to send him away. Eventually, the bishop asked that the Lady provide a sign; only then would he build the requested shrine.

Juan Diego returned to Our Lady. She told him to come back the following day and promised to give him a sign. But when Juan Diego returned home, he found his uncle, Juan Bernardino, stricken with fever. He spent the next day by his uncle's bedside, missing his appointment with Our Lady.

Juan Bernardino's condition turned critical, and Juan Diego left to find a priest to administer Last Rites. He chose a route that took him away from Tepeyac because he was embarrassed by his failure to fulfill Our Lady's request. He was trying to avoid her.

But the Blessed Mother found Juan Diego on his detour and greeted him not with anger but with love.

Listen and let it penetrate your heart, my dear little son, she told Juan Diego. Do not be troubled or weighted down with grief. Do not fear any illness or vexation, anxiety or pain. Am I not here who am your Mother?

Our Lady assured Juan Diego that his uncle was cured. Then she sent him to Tepeyac. At its summit, Juan Diego found the sign Our Lady had promised the bishop: a beautiful garden of flowers growing in the frozen soil, including Castilian roses.

Juan Diego gathered up the flowers and returned to Our Lady. She arranged them in a beautiful bouquet, placed them in his tilma, and told him not to reveal them until he stood before the bishop.

When Juan Diego returned to the bishop, he opened his cloak, and the beautiful Castilian roses dropped to the floor. The bishop dropped to his knees as well. He had received the very sign for which he had asked Our Lady.

The tilma of Guadalupe continues to confound scientists to this day, with its inexplicable durability, iridescence, lack of brush strokes, and tiny human figures in the Virgin's eyes, seemingly capturing the scene when the tilma was first unrolled by Juan Diego.

THE MIRACULOUS TILMA

The tilma of Guadalupe belongs to a category of religious artifacts known as *acheiropoieta,* meaning "made without hands." The name refers to icons and images believed to have come into existence miraculously, without a human artist. In addition to the tilma, other acheiropoieta include the Veil of Veronica, the Shroud of Turin, and the Image of Edessa, also known as the Mandylion.

The tilma has baffled scientists, who are unable to explain its longevity. Its rough cactus fibers should have decayed within a few decades of being woven; its colors should have faded long ago, as they have every time an artist has attempted replication. Yet the tilma, now nearly five hundred years old, continues to awe pilgrims with its beauty and freshness and vibrancy. An estimated ten million people come to see it each year.

The tilma has done more than survive the normal ravages of time. In 1785, a shrine worker accidentally doused the tilma with nitric acid. This should have destroyed the tilma almost instantly; instead, it self-restored over the following thirty days. And in 1921, an anticlerical activist launched a deliberate attack, detonating a powerful bomb directly in front of the tilma. Windows 150 feet away and a marble altar rail shattered, and a heavy brass crucifix was bent out of shape. The tilma, including the glass case that enclosed it, was untouched.

Closer examination of the tilma using scientific instruments only deepen the mystery. Nobel prize winning chemist Richard Kuhn discovered that the core image bore no trace of natural or animal colorings. Others have found no evidence of brush strokes, or of a priming treatment, or paint. Conclusion: The image was imprinted onto the tilma by unknown means, all at once.

Yet the roses were only half the miracle. For as Juan Diego opened his tilma, he revealed imprinted upon it a stunning image of a young mestiza woman, beautiful and gentle—an image that would come to be known as Our Lady of Guadalupe.

VIRGIN, MOTHER, AND QUEEN

Visitors to Mexico City today can still see what Bishop Zumarraga saw almost five hundred years ago. It is an image that has been venerated and examined for centuries, inspiring devotion and provoking wonder in people from all walks of life.

For the Aztecs, it had special meaning and resonance. They saw, for example, that the Lady in the image wore her hair straight down—a sign of virginity. Yet she was clearly pregnant, and the black belt around her waist was an Aztec symbol of maternity. She was both a virgin and a mother. And since she was being carried— held aloft as Aztec rulers were—by other's hands (by a small child angel seen at the bottom of the image), she was also a queen.

Here was the Woman who had appeared at Tepeyac, site of an old mother goddess shrine. Here though was the true mother, one far more powerful than the one for whom the Aztecs had built their shrine. She was the Woman of Revelation chapter 12, clothed with the sun and with the moon under her feet. Even Aztecs not familiar with Revelation could see that here was a woman from heaven, chiefly because of the stars that surrounded her.

And yet, she was not a goddess. Her eyes were cast down in humility, her hands folded in prayer. She was not cruel like the gods and goddesses of the Aztec pantheon. She was not demanding the lives of her people. Rather, she was coming to bring them something, or rather someone: the child present in her womb, whom they would soon come to know as Jesus Christ.

Within days of Juan Diego's gathering of the roses in his tilma, thousands were flocking to the site of the apparition. There the bishop had erected a small chapel. Two cultures that had once been at war now knelt together in prayer.

News of the miraculous image on Juan Diego's tilma spread all over Mexico. Artists painted replicas, and people carried the story with them wherever they went. They were captivated by the tenderness and humility of the Lady of Tepeyac and in awe of her power. She had worked great miracles among them: the miracle of the roses, the miracle of the tilma image, and miracles of healing with which the tilma quickly became associated.

She was clearly more powerful than their Aztec gods. Yet she did not point to herself. She pointed to her son, true God indeed, a God who offered hope to the terrorized and freedom to the enslaved, a God who did not demand the shedding of human blood through sacrificial acts, but rather made the ultimate sacrifice himself, pouring out his own blood for women and men.

The Aztecs who had been so slow to convert were won over. Estimates vary, but as many as nine million Aztecs entered the Church within twenty years of Mary's appearance to Juan Diego. It is said that one priest baptized over one million people with his own hands. Never before in history had there been such a mass conversion to the Faith.

The Lady of Tepeyac would go on to become the beloved patroness of the Mexican people. But she would come to be known under another title: Our Lady of Guadalupe.

It seemed an odd title for the mestizo woman on the tilma. Guadalupe was not an Aztec word, but a Spanish one; indeed, Guadalupe was the site of a Marian shrine in Spain, one familiar and beloved to many of the Spanish colonists.

But why would Our Lady reveal herself under this title, when appearing as a native woman in the New World?

The most likely answer is she did not. Guadalupe was probably a misconstrual by Bishop Zumarraga's interpreter of the name Our Lady gave herself in the native Aztec language. It was a happy coincidence because the word *Guadalupe* immediately attracted the excitement and interest of the Spaniards. But the name which

Our Lady gave herself was likely something that *sounded like* Guadalupe to Spanish ears but meant something entirely different to the Aztecs.

What name could that have been? One Aztec phrase that could easily be construed as *Guadalupe* by a Spanish speaker is *Coatlaxopeuh.* It's meaning? "She who crushes the serpent." Another possibility is *Tequantlaxopeuh,* which means "who saves us from the Devourer."

THE COURSE OF HISTORY CHANGED

It is impossible to tally the graces Our Lady of Guadalupe has brought, not just to the Mexican people, but to the world. Shrines have been built to Our Lady of Guadalupe in London, Italy, Poland, Nagasaki, the United States, and dozens of other countries. And of course there is still the main shrine in Mexico City, which welcomes some twenty million pilgrims a year.

All of this began with a simple peasant and the love he had for his spiritual mother. Juan Diego's example shows that each of us, no matter how little we are, can change the course of history.

And is there not so much that needs to be changed? We may not see human sacrifices atop pagan temples today, but we know the devil is still among us. One need only look at our modern culture to see his diabolical fingerprints.

Consider that before the Spanish conquistadores put a stop to the practice, the Aztecs sacrificed one out of every five of their children to their pagan gods. It is an astonishing statistic. But it should give us pause that today in the United States, one out of every four children are lost to abortion. The ways of the devil have changed, but his intentions remain the same.

Yet we mustn't lose hope. Our Lady will never abandon us. She will always be the merciful mother of all who love her, who cry to her, and who have confidence in her. She will ever draw us near to her Son, our Savior, so long as we remain, like Juan Diego, one of her humble little children.

LEFT
Many miracles have been associated with the tilma, including the raising of an Aztec man from the dead.

I Am the Immaculate Conception

CHAPTER 8

LEFT
At Lourdes, Our Lady revealed herself as the Immaculate Conception.

France is a land made holy by saints. Consider the names Joan of Arc, Vincent de Paul, Margaret Mary Alacoque, Francis de Sales, John Vianney, King Louis IX, Catherine Labouré, Louis de Montfort, and Thérèse of Lisieux. Few countries have set more jewels in the Church's crown than France.

But the sanctity of this nation would not keep her from being attacked by one of history's greatest evils. In fact, it is often the holiest who draw the fiercest gaze from the forces of darkness. By the envy of the devil, death entered the world (see Ws 2:24), and though this refers in the first instance to the Fall, it applies to countless other spiritual battlefields throughout history, where the devil has sought to wrest from nations, communities, and persons their greatest gift: friendship with God.

In the eighteenth century, the Church in France would become the prime target of a revolution that sought to tear her apart and rip out her very soul. Dogmas were doubted, altars desecrated, the faithful persecuted, and the blood of martyrs soaked the streets.

Yet, in the aftermath of these atrocities, the Mother of the Church would visit a humble young girl.

Bernadette Soubirous would one day stand in the hall of saints beside so many of her French brothers and sisters. And it would be the Immaculate Conception who ushered her in.

"ENLIGHTENED" ATTACKS

Late in the eighteenth century, most of France's twenty-eight million citizens owed their spiritual allegiance to Rome. But these bonds, stretching back over one thousand years, were on the verge of breaking.

The so-called Enlightenment, led by writers such as Voltaire and Jean Jacques Rousseau, had attacked the Church for decades, mocking religious faith and urging skepticism. The grim tenor of the movement could be summed up in a quote attributed to the famous Enlightenment writer Denis Diderot, who said, "Man will never be free until the last king is strangled with the entrails of the last priest."

In the summer of 1789, Diderot's dark vision began to materialize. The French National Assembly stared down King Louis XVI, eroding his power. Then it turned to the Church. In the months that followed, it would abolish Church tithes and seize Church property. The Revolution had begun.

By 1793, the Revolution had paved the way for the Reign of Terror. In a period of just fifteen months, forty thousand people were executed, including many clergy. Along the Nantes River, hundreds of priests were tied to rocks and tossed into the deep water to drown. And the heroic Carmelite nuns of Compiegne were beheaded at the guillotine as they sang the *Veni Creator Spiritus.*

The Church did not suffer mere physical violence; her very soul was under attack. The government launched a campaign of "dechristianization" with the goal of destroying the Church. Public worship was forbidden, and all visible signs of Christianity were removed—crosses and crucifixes, statues and works of art. Churches were closed and turned into warehouses or stables, or else converted into "temples of reason." A new calendar was even implemented, structured around the advent of the French Republic instead of the birth of Christ.

These were government sanctioned efforts to suppress religion. The malice of individuals and mobs was worse. Altars were desecrated and outrageous sacrileges were committed against the Blessed Sacrament. Church processions and Masses were interrupted with obscene displays and songs. Priests were hung in effigy. At the Notre Dame Cathedral in Paris, a prostitute was hailed as the goddess of reason and placed upon the high altar for mock veneration.

When Napoleon came to power in 1799, he sought to ease tensions between the French Republic and the Church. But he was power hungry and wanted the Church to bend to his will. In 1808, he occupied Rome and annexed the Papal States. When Pope Pius VII excommunicated him, Napoleon responded by seizing the pontiff and holding him hostage for six years.

The attacks on the Church during the Revolutionary and Napoleonic periods were so unprecedented one cannot help but see the fury of the devil behind them. St. John Paul II once com-

During the Reign of Terror, hundreds of priests were tied to rocks and tossed into the Nantes River to drown.

mented on the presence of Satan throughout history, saying it is "a presence which becomes all the more acute when man and society depart from God." France, the eldest daughter of the Church, had not only departed from God; she had tried to kill him. She had mocked the Faith in unspeakable ways and violently attacked those who professed their love of Christ.

The tumult of the Revolutionary and Napoleanic periods would subside, but the effects of the spiritual and physical assault on the Church would last for generations. When St. John Vianney was appointed the pastor, or *cure*, of the French village of Ars in 1818, he found his parish almost completely uncatechized. And when Bernadette Soubirous was born in 1844, France was still reeling from the Revolution's aftermath.

A HOUSE OF PRAYER

The village of Lourdes sits at the foothills of the Pyrenees Mountains in southern France. In the mid-nineteenth century, it was a simple mill town, full of peasants and ordinary people, with about four thousand inhabitants.

Just about everyone in Lourdes was poor, but perhaps the poorest of them all was the Soubirous family. St. Bernadette's family had to travel many times in order to find work, and Bernadette herself oftentimes had to leave her family to work as a shepherdess or as a maid. She would work so hard that she suffered from illness most of her life.

And yet of all this illness and suffering, what most embarrassed Bernadette was her lack of education. Bernadette's struggling family situation prevented her from attending school and catechism classes. And since she was not catechized, she could not make her first Communion. Of all her trials, this is what gave the saint her greatest sorrow and shame.

By 1856, when Bernadette was twelve, the family was forced to move to find work. The situation was dire. They had to live in a place called the Rue du Bourg, up against the rock of the local castle that overlooked the village. It was a little hovel called "the dungeon." It was actually a structure that was once used as a jail.

It was a hard life, but the family never failed to pray each night. They would gather in their shadowy dungeon of a home with only the light of a fire to illuminate a crucifix hanging on a wall with a rosary draped around it, and before these sacred objects, they would pray.

LADY FROM HEAVEN

Thursday, February 11, 1858 was a dreary and bitterly cold day. Fourteen-year-old Bernadette, her sister, and a friend journeyed to a rocky crag at the foot of the Pyrenees Mountains, known as Massabielle, to gather firewood. Here the Gave River washed up driftwood. It was a lonely, abandoned place, often called the pigsty because a local swineherd would use it as a watering hole.

When they arrived at the pigsty, Bernadette's sister and friend crossed the icy stream to search for wood. As Bernadette remained alone, she heard a powerful gust of wind, as if a storm were approaching. A moment later, she saw *her*.

At first, Bernadette didn't know who was visiting her. She was so innocent and humble it never occurred to her that this beautiful Woman might be the Mother of God. She was actually afraid. She reached into her pocket and grabbed her rosary. She was comforted when she saw the Woman had a rosary of her own, following along on the beads silently with Bernadette.

The beautiful Lady vanished after Bernadette finished praying. Moments later, her sister and friend returned to find her pale and unresponsive. Bernadette eventually told them what she saw. Though the two girls promised to say nothing, soon the whole town knew of the strange occurrences at Massabielle.

Bernadette's parents were understandably worried. They didn't want her to go back. Some local sisters and priests advised

Bernadette was so innocent and humble it never occurred to her that this beautiful Woman might be the Mother of God.

Photograph of Marie Lemarchand (ABOVE LEFT) after her miraculous cure at Lourdes. Before the miracle, Emile Zola (ABOVE RIGHT) wrote that Lemarchand "looked hideously like a monster" due to lupus and ulcers ravaging her face.

ÉMILE ZOLA AND THE MIRACLE AT LOURDES

In the late 1800s, Émile Zola was perhaps the most famous novelist in France. As the founder of the literary school of naturalism, Zola's novels paint a grim world devoid of God and grace, where belief in prayer or miracles are delusions doomed to futility.

In 1892, Zola turned his attention to Lourdes. In August, he set out to conduct first-hand research for a novelized exposé of the Shrine. Along the way, he encountered an eighteen-year-old woman named Marie Lemarchand. Marie, her body ravaged by tuberculosis, lupus, and ulcers, was traveling to Lourdes as well.

Zola recoiled on seeing her face. Part of Marie's nose and mouth had been eaten away by disease. "The whole was a frightful distorted mass of matter and oozing blood," he would write later.

At Lourdes, Marie entered the baths and rose from the water instantaneously cured. Zola was present when Marie emerged. He saw her cure and knew it endured (she would go on to marry and have eight children). But when Zola placed Marie in his novel *Lourdes,* as the character Elise Rouquet, he made her a vain figure, perhaps ill only through hysteria, with the persistence of her healing in doubt.

Zola had traveled to Lourdes purporting to have an open mind. But after seeing Marie's miracle, and even another first hand, he remained steadfast in disbelief. "Were I to see all the sick at Lourdes cured," he would say, "I would not believe in a miracle."

her not to either, or even to talk about what she had seen. But Bernadette felt impelled to return to Massabielle. She convinced her parents that the vision couldn't be dangerous because she had held a rosary. Bernadette's parents relented. She returned to Massabielle on Sunday, February 14.

At this second apparition, there were about twenty people present with Bernadette. Although they could not see the Lady, they could see Bernadette in ecstasy. When the Lady came, Bernadette asked her whether she was from God. Then she sprinkled holy water on the rocks below the Woman's feet.

The Lady smiled. It was the first sign that she was from heaven. Bernadette remained in an ecstasy so profound that later a friend of the family, a grown man, had to pick her up in order to carry her home.

After the second vision, word spread even more, and Bernadette's parents grew even more upset. But Bernadette again felt impelled to return to her grotto.

She was allowed to return a third time with two adult friends of the family to chaperone her. Just as before, the Lady appeared, but Bernadette was the only one who could see her. Still, the two women said they felt a presence there, and the young girl's face was enraptured.

It was at this third apparition that the Lady spoke for the first time. She asked Bernadette to return each day for a fortnight. And she spoke to Bernadette words that hinted both at future suffering and a crown of glory beyond it: *I do not promise to make you happy in this life, but in the next.*

Bernadette journeyed to Massabielle each day for the next two weeks as the Lady had asked. The crowds followed. Skeptical clergy and journalists came and even a doctor who monitored Bernadette in hopes of proving she was delusional.

But all who watched her knew she was seeing *something.* It was in her eyes, they said; the look from her eyes alone was enough to bring them to their knees.

LEFT
Our Lady told Bernadette: *I do not promise to make you happy in this life, but in the next.*

Whatever it was that Bernadette saw, the forces of evil were put on watch, sensing that this Lady had come to set sinners free. On one occasion, as the Lady stood before Bernadette, the young girl heard a clamoring of vicious voices coming from the caves behind the bright vision. One of these sinister voices was more dominant than the rest, screaming *Get out! Get out! Leave!* Bernadette realized with dread that these were no human voices, but those of demons. Their anger, spite, and hatred were directed not just to her but also to the Lady.

But the dread did not last long. The Lady simply turned and gave a look of authority in the direction of the voices. They immediately went silent. The devil and his minions were not going to drive the Lady from that place no matter how hard they tried.

SPRING OF HEALING

On February 25, the day of the ninth apparition, the Lady told Bernadette she should drink at the "fountain," pointing to a little puddle under a rock. Bernadette obeyed, scooping up the muddy water, digging with her hands to find some that was fresh.

She must have made an odd sight: a poor, uneducated little girl on her knees, digging in the mud in response to a vision no one else could see. There were hundreds of people in the crowd that day. Many of them must have seen Bernadette as a poster child for the Enlightenment's ridicule of religion.

But what began as a trickle of muddy water beneath the clawing hands of a little girl became a spring that flows to this day, a spring where millions have come for hope and healing.

The very first healing happened just days later when a local woman regained the use of her paralyzed arm after bathing it in the spring. Many more would follow. Today, the Shrine of Lourdes has files on nearly seven thousand unexplained cures. After rigorous investigation, the Church has declared sixty-nine of them miraculous.

The heroic Carmelite
nuns of Compiegne
were beheaded
at the guillotine as
they sang the *Veni
Creator Spiritus*.

The apparitions continued until, at the end of February, the Lady made a request of Bernadette. She wanted a chapel built. Bernadette petitioned the local clergy, but was sent away. She persisted, not wanting to fail the beautiful Lady.

The matter was eventually laid before a very gruff parish priest, Abbe Peyramale, who demanded to know the Lady's name. Up to this point Bernadette had not claimed that the Lady was Mary. She had asked the Lady her name on several occasions, but all the Lady did in reply was smile.

Finally, toward the end of March, on the feast of the Annunciation, Bernadette asked again and received a reply: *I am the Immaculate Conception.*

Bernadette had no idea what this meant, but she was elated at having finally gotten her answer. She ran to tell Abbe Peyramale, repeating the phrase over and over again so as to not forget it.

Just four years earlier, in 1854, Pius IX had infallibly declared the dogma of Mary's immaculate conception. In choosing this title for herself at Lourdes, Mary was doing two things. First, she was pointing to the authority of the pope. His authority had been severely undermined by the Revolution and Napoleon. But here we see heaven itself listening to and repeating his decree. Second, she was pointing to the power of faith. The simple, uneducated Bernadette, through faith, was "enlightened" to a truth to which skeptical intellectuals were blind.

The revelation that the Lady of Lourdes identified herself as the Immaculate Conception, together with the miraculous cures from the spring at the grotto, brought belief and legitimacy to Bernadette's claims. Eventually, the chapel was built. Lourdes would become a pilgrimage site for millions.

Bernadette's life soon returned to normal, as normal as the life of a seer could be. She joined the Sisters of Charity in Nevers, France, and lived out her life in their convent. And when she left this world, she did so with one more miracle that would confound the skeptics: Her body remained incorrupt and can be visited and venerated by pilgrims to this day.

THE CHURCH REVIVED

Our Lady's appearance at Lourdes happened at a time when the Church was ridiculed and attacked. The blood of martyrs had been spilled, Church teaching doubted, and altars desecrated. Reason had become the god of the world, and the smug leaders of the Enlightenment scoffed at taverns all over France at the mad little girl kneeling in her grotto.

But Mary's appearances at Lourdes, coupled with Bernadette's witness of faith, helped revive the Church in France. In the span of just a century, France would go from beheading Carmelite nuns at the guillotine to reading en masse the spiritual memoir of a young Carmelite named Thérèse, making *Story of a Soul* the best-selling book in the country.

The Lady of the Rosary

––––– M –––––

CHAPTER

9

LEFT
The Lady told the
three children not
to be afraid, that she
came from heaven.

On October 13, 1884, Pope Leo XIII turned pale and collapsed just after celebrating Mass. Those with him rushed to his side, fearing him dead. But when he regained consciousness, he said he'd been given a vision of Satan before the throne of God, boasting that he could destroy the Church.

When God replied that his Church was everlasting, incapable of destruction, the devil asked for a century of power in which to prove his claim. According to Pope Leo's vision, Our Lord granted Satan these one hundred years.

Pope Leo then saw wars, immorality, persecution, and genocide on a mass scale, dark omens of what was to come. When the vision ended and he regained consciousness, he rushed to his chambers. There he penned the now-famous prayer to St. Michael, calling upon the warrior angel to cast down to hell the devil and his demons.

Though the Church has never confirmed this account, the horrific events of the twentieth century may lead us to believe that the devil *has* been granted great power in these modern times—two world wars, a holocaust, debauchery and immorality celebrated on a massive scale, and confusion, corruption, and an erosion of faith even within the Church. And let us not forget that the twentieth century saw more martyrs than all the previous centuries combined.

We may wonder why the Lord would allow the devil such a reign of terror. But we know that, as the phoenix rises from the ashes, the Church rises anew from the blood of the martyrs. It is the darkest ages that produce the greatest saints. And, as at other times in history, the dangers and perils would prompt the Queen of Heaven to leave her throne and call her children back to God.

What follows is an account of events that altered the course of the twentieth century. These events brought light and hope to a violent and troubled period. And they showed our Mother fighting for our salvation yet again, freeing us from the grasp of the devil.

If the story of Leo's vision is true, and it did in fact happen on October 13, 1884, then that would give special significance to what would happen thirty-three years later on that very same date when Our Lady made the sun dance over the skies of Portugal.

THE ANGEL OF PEACE

Fatima is a small village that lies amid the rugged, pine-clad ranges of the Serra d'Aire Mountains of central Portugal. It is a quiet place, unassuming and modest. But as we have seen, it is so often in these hidden and forgotten places where miraculous events occur.

Our Lady would proclaim a message of peace to the world from the quiet hills of Fatima, drowning out the war cries reverberating around the globe. And she chose to deliver this message to three children as unlikely as the little town they called home.

Lucia Santos, the eldest of the three, and her two cousins, Fernando and Jacinta Marto, spent their days tending flocks in the pastures. Their families were poor but devout. It was a difficult time to be Catholic. The Church in Portugal was being persecuted by Marxists and freemason anarchists, priests were being exiled or told not to wear their clerical dress, churches and monasteries were turned into barracks and government offices, and holy days were secularized.

Mary was not the first heavenly visitor to the children. In 1916, the year before Mary's appearances, an angel appeared to them. He introduced himself as the Angel of Peace, and he asked the children to make reparation to God for the offenses of mankind. The angel visited three times, and on his last visit, he brought the children Holy Communion.

The Angel of Peace appeared to the three children in the spring of 1916, just two years after the start of World War I. Nearly one hundred million military personnel were engaged in battle all across Europe. Twenty million would die in the violence, and entire cities would be reduced to rubble.

At no other time in history had the world been in more desperate need of peace. At Fatima, heaven would disclose a plan to bring it.

The dazzled crowd watched as the sun made strange and abrupt movements.

THE APPARITIONS

The Cova da Iria was a field, a vast natural hollow owned by the Santos family, just over a mile from their home. It was a lonely place, overrun by brush and foliage because of its infrequent use. The children brought their flocks to this field on May 13, 1917. They said their Rosary, as they were accustomed to doing, and began to play. But soon a vivid flash of light overwhelmed them.

Though the day was clear, they thought at first that a storm was approaching. Then they saw her, the Lady, amidst a dazzling light, resting atop a small holm oak tree. She wore a white mantle that fell to her feet, and a star shone from the hem of her robe. In her hands, she held a sparkling rosary. She told them not to be afraid, that she came from heaven. But she didn't reveal who she was.

All three children saw the Lady, but each had a different experience. Jacinta could see and hear her, but could not speak back, while Francisco could only see her, but not hear her. Lucia was the only one who could see her, hear her, and communicate with her. When the Lady asked the children if they would offer themselves to God and accept all the sufferings he might send them, to make reparation for the sins of mankind and for the conversion of sinners, Lucia was the one who consented on behalf of the others.

The Lady said they would each have much to suffer. Then she told them she would return on the thirteenth day of the month for six consecutive months, after which she would reveal who she was.

Lucia advised her younger cousins not to speak of the vision to anyone, but they could not contain their excitement. Jacinta and Francisco told their parents about the vision that very night, and soon the whole town knew about it.

Lucia's mother was irate. Maria Santos was a very strict woman, and she was intent on raising God-fearing children. She

thought her daughter was spreading lies and demanded Lucia renounce what she had said. When Lucia refused, her mother punished her. This would be a great source of pain and suffering for Lucia, her own mother's anger and disbelief.

Many of the townspeople disbelieved them as well; the children were ridiculed, even spat on. Still, when it came time for the next visit from the Lady, several dozen others came with them to the Cova da Iria.

On June 13 in 1917, Our Lady appeared to the children a second time. This time the children were not alone. There were other people present, and while they didn't see Mary, they did see the cloud on which she stood.

Mary emphasized again the need of prayer, especially the Rosary. Lucia jumped in and said, "I want to go to heaven now."

Mary made it understood that the other two children, Francisco and Jacinta, would actually be coming to heaven shortly, but Lucia would remain for a long time to spread devotion to the Immaculate Heart.

Lucia must have been scared. She didn't want to be alone, but Mary assured her that her Immaculate Heart would always be with her.

After this second visit, word spread even more. People were speaking about how the cloud was seen by everyone, not just the children, and that the branches of the holm oak tree were bent back, as if someone had been standing on it.

Lucia's mother was beside herself. She took Lucia to the parish priest to be straightened out. He speculated that it all might have been a manifestation of the devil. Lucia was horrified, and resolved to stay away from the field, and even from her cousins. But the Holy Spirit instilled in her an overwhelming desire to return when the day of the apparitions arrived the next month.

On July 13, the children went again to the Cova da Iria. Word had continued to spread, and this time, five thousand others went with the three children. Again, witnesses saw the small cloud descending from the eastern sky, but they could not see the Lady. She appeared to the children and urged them to pray the Rosary every day so that peace would come to the war-torn world.

THE SECRET OF FATIMA

Lucia asked for a miracle so that the people could believe. The Lady promised to deliver a miracle in October at the end of the six months. But on this apparition, she would give the children something else: a secret. It would come to be known as the secret of Fatima, a secret made up of three parts.

The first part was a vision of hell, communicating its reality and its danger to souls. Lucia would later write about the vision in her memoirs. The description was chilling:

O MILAGRE DE FÁTIMA

Varios aspectos do povo ajoelhado e orando no momento de descobrir o sol e de se dar o fenomeno que tanto impressionou a multidão.

no vagalhão colossal d'aquele povo que ali se juntou a 13 de outubro. O teu racionalismo sofreu um formidavel embate e quer-s estabelecer uma opinião segura socorrendo-te de depoimentos insuspeitos como o meu, pois que estive lá apenas no desempenho de uma missão bem dificil, tal a de relatar imparcialmente para um grande diario, *O Seculo*, os factos que diante de mim se desenrolassem e tudo quanto de curioso e de elucidativo a eles se prendesse. Não ficará por satisfazer o teu desejo, mas decerto que os nossos olhos e os nossos ouvidos não viram nem ouviram coisas diversas, e que raros foram os que ficaram insensiveis á grandeza de semelhante espectaculo, unico entre nós e de todo o ponto digno de meditação e de estudo ..

* * *

[Carta a alguem que pede um testemunho insuspeito].

Quebrando um silencio de mais de vinte anos e com a invocação dos longinquos e saudosos tempos em que convivemos n'uma fraternal camaradagem, iluminada então pla fé comum e fortalecida por identicos propositos, escreves-me para que te diga, sincera e minuciosamente, o que vi e ouvi na chrneca de Fátima, quando a fama de celestes aparições congregou n'aquele desolado ermo dezenas de milhares de pessoas mais sedentas, segundo creio, de sobrenatural do que impelidas por mera curiosidade ou receosas de um logro... Estão os catolicos em desacordo sobre a importancia e a significação do que presenciaram. Uns convenceram-se de que se tinham cumprido prometimentos do Alto; outros acham-se ainda longe de acreditar na incontroversa realidade de um milagre. Foste um crente na tua juventude e deixaste de sel-o. Pessoas de familia arrastaram-te a Fátima,

O que ouvi e me levou a Fátima? Que a Virgem Maria, depois da festa da Ascenção, aparecera a tres crianças que apascentavam gado, duas mocinhas e um zagalete, recomendando-lhes que orassem e prometendo-lhes aparecer ali, sobre uma azinheira, no dia 13 de cada mez, até em outubro lhes daria qualquer sinal do poder de Deus e faria revelações. Espalhou-se a nova por muitas leguas em redonde; voou, de terra em terra, até os confins de Portugal, e a roma-

555

WITNESSES TO THE
MIRACLE OF THE SUN

Many miracles have occurred in Church history. But as a public and spectacular demonstration of God's power, nothing since Biblical times compares to Fatima's miracle of the sun. In the days following the miracle on October 13, 1917, it was front page news in Catholic and anti-Catholic newspapers alike, both in Portugal and abroad.

Avelino de Almeida was one of the witnesses of the miracle. Editor of the anticlerical newspaper *O Seculo*, he had mocked the Fatima apparitions in writing. His tone would be far different in his column of October 15th. Headlining his column *How the sun danced in broad daylight at Fátima*, he described the event as follows:

> "We saw the huge crowd turn towards the sun which appeared at its zenith, clear of the clouds. It resembled a flat plate of silver, and it was possible to stare at it without the least discomfort. It did not burn the eyes. It did not blind. We would say that it produced an eclipse. Then a tremendous cry rang out. . . *Miracle! Miracle! Marvel! Marvel!*

O Portugal, another anticlerical paper, would also testify to the miracle on the front page of its October 15th edition. The paper described the sun moving "like a mad dancer in a wild country dance" and complained that the Fatima seers (whom the paper called "three boorish children") had come along and overturned scientific truth.

We could see a vast sea of fire. Plunged in the flames were demons and lost souls, as if they were red-hot coals, transparent and black or bronze-colored, in human form, which floated about in the conflagration without weight or equilibrium, amid shrieks and groans of sorrow and despair that horrified us and caused us to tremble with fear. The devils could be distinguished by horrible and loathsome forms of animals, frightful and unknown, but transparent like black coals that have turned red-hot.[7]

The Lady then explained what they had seen. *You have seen hell where the souls of poor sinners go. In order to save them, God wishes to establish in the world devotion to my Immaculate Heart.*

The second part of the secret foretold the end of the current war and the threat of a larger one. *The war is going to end,* said the Lady. *But if people do not stop offending God, another, even worse, will begin. When you see a night illumined by an unknown light,* the Lady continued, *know that this is the great sign given you by God that he is about to punish the world for its crimes, by means of war, famine, and persecutions of the Church and of the Holy Father.*

To prevent or mitigate the suffering that loomed on the horizon, Our Lady asked for two things: for the pope and bishops to consecrate Russia to her Immaculate Heart and for the spread of the Five First Saturdays devotion. *If my requests are heeded,* said the Lady, *Russia will be converted, and there will be peace; if not, she will spread her errors throughout the world, raising up wars and persecutions against the Church. The good will be martyred, the Holy Father will suffer much, and various nations will be annihilated.*

For the third part of the secret, Our Lady showed the children yet another haunting vision, one involving the assassination of a "bishop dressed in white." Lucia and the children did not reveal this part of the secret publicly. Lucia, in obedience to the

LEFT
The devils could be distinguished by horrible and loathsome forms of animals, frightful and unknown.

---

[7] Sister Maria Lucia of the Immaculate Heart, *Fatima in Lucia's Own Words: The Memoirs of Sister Lucia, the Last Fatima Visionary.* Kindle edition *(KIC, 2015)*.

bishop of Leira, Portugal, wrote it down in 1944, but it would not be revealed for many years.

THE MIRACLE OF THE SUN

After the July apparition, the children were detained by the local authorities and questioned. The anti-Catholic authorities were enraged that three illiterate shepherd children were riling up the pious faithful. The mayor was also obsessed with discovering the details of the secret, which the children hadn't revealed yet.

The mayor kidnapped the children on August 13 so they couldn't go to the pasture. He even threatened to kill them and dip them in burning oil, but the children remained courageous and strong and said nothing. They recited the Rosary in their prison cell, and the other prisoners joined in.

Though the children were not able to meet the Lady for the apparition on the thirteenth, a crowd of fifteen thousand gathered. As news spread of the kidnapping, a surge of anger arose from within the crowd. They were on the verge of rioting when a violent clap of thunder stunned them.

Witnesses said the thunder was so loud they thought the world was ending. A flash of light followed, and then the same cloud as usual descended upon the tree. It remained for a few minutes before rising into the heavens.

Then everyone's faces shone bright with lots of colors, like a rainbow, and the tree's leaves appeared to morph into flowers. It seemed to be a sign to the faithful of the truth of the children's testimony—and of heaven's anger at their treatment.

Eventually the mayor relented and set the children free. Days later, the Lady came to Lucia and her cousins again. She implored them to pray and make sacrifices for sinners. She still promised the October miracle but said its greatness would be diminished because the authorities had treated the children so poorly.

Finally, October 13 arrived, the day of the promised mira-

The Angel of Peace
asked the children to
make reparation to
God for the offenses
of mankind.

cle. Over seventy thousand people, believers and doubters alike, swarmed into the Cova da Iria behind the children. Rain saturated the land all morning. At midday, the Lady appeared.

On this final visit, the Lady identified herself as Our Lady of the Rosary. She delivered one last somber message, a warning against offending the Lord, already so greatly offended by sin.

Mary disappeared, and the children saw St. Joseph with the Child Jesus. Then she reappeared, first as Our Lady of Sorrows and then as Our Lady of Carmel. These three visions have been thought by many to be symbols of the three sets of mysteries of the Rosary: the Joyful, represented with Joseph and the Child Jesus; the Sorrowful, represented by the Lady of Sorrows; and the Glorious, represented by Our Lady of Carmel. This would give meaning to the title the Lady gave herself at this moment: the Lady of the Rosary.

But while the children were gazing upon these visions, the crowd was witnessing something else. The seventy thousand people at the Cova de Iria saw the sun begin to spin and then dance in the sky. Then it appeared to plummet toward earth, and the crowd fell to its knees in terror and prayed to God for forgiveness. The sun returned to its normal position, and the crowd rose from its knees. Despite the earlier rain and the heavy mud, everyone was dry and clean.

When people would later reflect on the miracle of that day, many could not help but see heaven pointing to "the woman clothed with the sun" from the Book of Revelation, a woman in conflict with a great dragon seeking to devour her child (see Rv 12).

It was this very dragon who had been sweeping across the globe, terrorizing Mary's children with wars and persecutions.

Despite the wondrous display over the skies of Portugal that day, few would heed the warnings of Our Lady to pray and offer sacrifices for sinners. Few would make the Five First Saturdays. Her call for prayer and penance, simple acts that require no special talents, blessings, or riches, proved too much for so many.

Although the Great War would end, her prophecy of a new, far greater war would prove true. Even the omen, the light in the night sky, came to pass when, on January 25 and 26, 1938, an extraordinary aurora borealis lit up the skies of Europe and America. Lucia, by then a grown woman and religious sister, interpreted this as the sign Our Lady had prophesied. Less than two months after these brilliant lights painted the blackened firmament, German troops marched on Austria and annexed it. These were the seeds of World War II.

Our Lady told the children that this war would be far worse than the first, and again her words proved true. The Second World War claimed twice as many people, and an entire people were nearly extinguished from the earth.

There was still the matter of the Fatima secrets. The second war proved devastating. But what of Russia spreading her errors throughout the world? What of the bishop in white who was clearly in grave danger?

Many decades would pass before the full meaning of these dramatic secrets would become clear. What was certain, though, is that the end of World War II was not the end of danger, for the Church or the world. The devil would press his attack all the more fiercely as his century of dominion wound to a close. But heaven offered a refuge in the Immaculate Heart of Mary, and a humble Polish man who would lead the world within it.

My Immaculate Heart Will Triumph

CHAPTER

10

LEFT
"The bishop in white" had a strong devotion to Our Lady of Fatima.

The man they called John Paul headed towards the square in his open-air popemobile. Thousands of his flock were tucked within the Bernini colonnades that arched out as a symbol of the Church's maternal arms.

But a shark lurked within the sea of people. He had navigated the currents of the globe, passing undetected through the borders of Bulgaria, Switzerland, Austria, and Germany. Strapped close to his chest was a nine-millimeter Browning semiautomatic.

He waited patiently, hiding amidst the faithful, until his target drew close. When the motorcade got within just feet, he pulled the pistol from his jacket and pointed it at the bishop of Rome.

What happened next sent shockwaves across the world. But to understand the events of that day, we must return to the small pasture in Fatima where, sixty-four years prior, the Lady who would make the sun dance first appeared to the three shepherd children.

She had altered the course of history with her visit. Now, some would argue, she would alter the course of the bullet fired from the Browning semiautomatic.

RUSSIA SPREADS HER ERRORS

At Fatima, Our Lady had warned that a global war and the persecution of the Church were imminent. But men and women neglected her call to penance and prayer. Few would take refuge within her Immaculate Heart; few would pray the Rosary and offer sacrifices for sinners.

And so her proclamations came to pass. The world was again torn apart by war, and a new power arose in the East. Russia, as Mary had warned, began spreading her errors throughout the world.

At the time of Mary's warnings in 1917, the Russian Revolution had just begun. Turmoil was brewing. Still, few could have foreseen what would follow in the next seven decades. Russia, known as "Holy Russia," was a poor nation in 1917. The transformation of Holy Russia into the Soviet Union, with its atheistic communism, killings, Iron Curtain, and invasions all over eastern Europe was virtually unthinkable.

After the Revolution, Josef Stalin came to power. He enacted the Great Purge to remove those he thought opposed him and the Communist Party. People were detained, put in labor camps, and killed. Stalin was a staunch atheist, and his Soviet government promoted atheism through the schools and propaganda. He established antireligious laws and launched a campaign of terror against believers.

With most of Europe devastated by the war, Russia took advantage of a power vacuum, rebuilding its economy and assisting eastern European nations in their postwar recovery efforts. In the process, these smaller nations were turned into Soviet satellite states.

In the 1950s and 60s, the Soviet Union expanded its control, invading nations including Hungary, Poland, Latvia, Lithuania, Yugoslavia, and Romania. The Berlin Wall was built in 1961. Huge areas of historic Christendom were subjugated and repressed. Churches and schools were closed, priests were arrested, and the bishops behind the Iron Curtain in Soviet-controlled territories could not unite with the pope. Millions of Catholics were cut off from the rest of the Church and the outside world.

Russia's former allies, the United States and Great Britain, watched with grave concern. There may not have been a direct military conflict, but a Cold War arose between the American-led Western democracies and the Soviet Union, each side armed to the hilt.

Both powers had large arsenals of nuclear weapons, and people all over the world lived in fear of nuclear war. The United States felt this threat most acutely during the Cuban Missile Crisis, but there were people on other side of the world who felt the threat every single day. They, more than anyone else, could see the warnings of Fatima being played out on a daily basis.

Of all the eastern European nations to fall to the Soviets, one in particular became a thorn stuck in the side of the giant beast. Poland had shown its resolve against its mighty neighbor in the past, pushing back the spread of Lenin's revolution in 1920 on the banks of the Vistula River. Years later, the Soviet Union would have its revenge. The Poles eventually fell under Communist control after World War II. But just as before, this small nation found a way to win its freedom, thanks in large part to one of its native sons.

A MAN NAMED KAROL

Karol Wojtyla was born in 1920 in the Polish town of Wadowice. He had a difficult childhood: a sister died in childbirth, a brother died young, and his mother died when he was only eight. This early loss of his mother would lead to his strong devotion to Mary.

His father eventually moved them to Krakow where Karol thrived. He was athletic, intelligent, and popular. He spoke several languages and loved the arts. But in 1939, the Nazis invaded

The Poles fell under
Communist control
after WWII. But native
son Karol Wojtyla
would free them.

ABOVE
Lech Walesa said it was
impossible not to bow
before the champion of
the cause of freedom:
John Paul II

and everything changed. His university closed, and he was forced to work at a limestone quarry and a chemical factory in order to avoid deportation to Germany. When his father died of a heart attack in 1941, he was left without any family. That was when he began to seriously consider the priesthood.

In October of 1942, as the war raged on, Karol Wojtyla entered a clandestine underground seminary. In the shadows of Krakow, under the constant threat of imprisonment and death, he took his first steps toward the Chair of Peter.

He had lost his family, his country, and many friends, but his faith could not be shaken. His faith propelled him toward the priesthood, helped him survive German raids, and inspired him to save the lives of several Polish Jews.

The Germans fled Poland at the close of 1945. Less than three months later, Karol was ordained. His unique combination of intellect, charity, piety, and charisma made him immensely popular with his long-suffering Polish flock.

He spent most of his early priesthood in Krakow, teaching at the university. He gained a following of young people who adored him. It began with about a dozen before swelling to hundreds. They did everything together, from outdoor masses and helping the poor and sick, to writing and performing plays and going skiing in the mountains.

But though the war was over and the Nazis had left, things weren't easy. The Polish Communists had helped Stalin and the Soviet Union gain control, and they were hostile to the Church. Education in Poland was beginning to follow a Soviet model, trying to expose young people to the Communist propaganda and keep them from the Church. The group of young people had to call Karol "uncle" in public so the authorities wouldn't know he was a priest.

In 1958, Karol was elected auxiliary bishop of Krakow, becoming the youngest bishop in Polish history. Nine years later, he was elected to the College of Cardinals.

Even still, the papacy must have seemed beyond the realm of plausibility for him. Surely a native of Poland, a conquered nation trapped behind the Iron Curtain, could never become the spiritual father of Christ's Church. And yet this was what Providence designed.

After the death of Paul VI in 1978, John Paul I was elected, but his papacy would last only a matter of weeks before he suffered a sudden heart attack. A new conclave was called. Other candidates may have seemed more likely than the cardinal from Poland, but the Holy Spirit would oversee the election of Karol Wojtyla to the papacy on October 16, 1978. He took the name John Paul II in honor of his predecessor; he was the first non-Italian pope in almost five hundred years.

The Polish people were ecstatic. Their hopes were rejuvenated by the election to the papacy of one of their own. The Soviet reaction was different; in the Kremlin, there was all-out panic.

Pope John Paul II talks with his attempted assassin, Mehmet Ali Ağca. Ağca,
like Pope John Paul II, was convinced that Our Lady of Fatima had miraculously
intervened in the shooting to save John Paul's life.

THE POPE AND THE ASSASSIN

On December 27, 1983, Pope John Paul II traveled to Rome's Rebibbia Prison to visit its most famous inmate. Mehmet Ali Ağca, the man who 2½ years earlier had shot him in a failed assassination attempt, knelt and kissed the pope's ring.

John Paul had publicly forgiven Ağca right after he was shot. Now he was extending forgiveness personally.

The two men sat and talked quietly for twenty minutes. "I spoke to him as I would speak to a brother," the pope would say later. Several times he enclosed Ağca's hands in his own.

One question haunted Ağca. "So why aren't you dead?" A professional assassin, Ağca had shot John Paul four times at near point blank range. How had he survived?

John Paul said he had been protected by Our Lady of Fatima, whose feast day marked the assassination attempt. It was she who had guided the bullets, averting his death.

Ağca was terrified. He had seen the power of this "goddess of Fatima" first hand. Would she come to his prison cell and take her revenge?

No, the pope assured him. The Lady forgave him, as did he.

The Italian government released Ağca from prison in 2000 at John Paul's request. He served an additional ten years in Turkey for an earlier murder before being freed for good. Thirty-one years to the day after John Paul visited him in prison, Ağca traveled to Rome and laid flowers on his tomb.

Today he still has a fascination with the Lady of Fatima. But, as he said in an interview on Italian television, he knows her now as "the Madonna, my spiritual mother."[8]

---

[8] "Would-be papal assassin says he wants to be a priest," *Crux* (July 12, 2016)

The Soviet state had always kept the Catholic Church in its sights. The Church was a threat to the Soviets. She couldn't be bullied into changing her teachings. And she had international influence and unyielding dogmas opposed to the Soviet's atheistic creed.

The Church in Russia had been crushed in the 1930s. But from a global standpoint, the Church was still beyond Soviet control. Now, with the election of John Paul II as pope, there was a surge of hope and patriotism in Poland.

The Soviets warned the Vatican that if it tried to exercise influence in the East, Catholics behind the Iron Curtain would pay. But John Paul wasn't intimidated. He decided to go right into the fray. He decided to go home.

THE TRIP THAT CHANGED THE WORLD

During his pontificate, Pope John Paul traveled more than 650,000 miles and visited more than one hundred countries. He spoke to millions and walked in places no other pope had ever been. But among all his travels, his trip home to Poland in June of 1979, less than a year after his election, stands out.

It was a historic visit; no other pope had ever been to Poland. The Communist Party was in a dilemma about letting him come. To deny him might signal to the world that they were afraid of him and afraid of Rome, plus they might have angry mobs to deal with. On the other hand, his visit might inspire a revolution.

In the end, they let him come, knowing it would be too big of a global embarrassment to shun the pope. But they took measures to blunt his influence. They had schoolteachers tell children John Paul was their enemy, that he was trying to brainwash them, and they censored the media throughout his visit, even going so far as to only show clergy, the elderly, and sick or handicapped people in the crowds that came out to see him. And if there was an uprising, they planned to blame him for inciting violence.

LEFT
John Paul wasn't intimidated by the Soviets. He decided to go right into the fray. He decided to go home.

The government feared hundreds of thousands of people would come out to see him. By the end of the trip, across several different cities, it's estimated thirteen million took to the streets to see their beloved Papa. A million people attended his Mass in Victory Square in Warsaw alone.

Standing beneath a fifty-foot-tall cross, John Paul II gave an inspiring homily that touched on the sufferings of the Polish people and said that God had a great role for them to fulfill. When he asked if they were up to such a task, the people began to chant. Shouts of *We want God! We want God!* boomed from the crowd.

Many commentators point to the pope's homecoming as the beginning of the end of the Soviet Union. Millions of Poles came out of hiding to join the Solidarity movement, a nonviolent, anticommunist labor and trade union founded by the courageous Lech Walesa. The movement was invigorated by John Paul's visit and a peaceful revolution against the Soviet state was born.

But the battle was not yet over. Soon the evil empire would have their revenge on this bishop dressed in white.

SHOTS IN THE SQUARE

May 13, 1981, sixty-four years to the day after the children of Fatima first saw the mysterious Lady standing atop the holm oak, John Paul II prepared for his weekly audience in St. Peter's Square.

The previous night, John Paul had read a verse from the New Testament as part of his Compline prayers: "Be sober, be watchful. Your adversary the devil prowls around like a roaring lion, seeking some one to devour" (1 Pt 5:8).

As he entered the Square in his open-air popemobile, he encountered a crowd of nearly twenty thousand cheering pilgrims. He greeted them warmly, stopping to bless individuals on his way to the podium where he would deliver his address. He had just blessed a little girl and was nearing the Bronze Doors of the

Apostolic Palace when the sound of gunfire changed the cheering of the pilgrims to screams.

Four shots had been fired in rapid succession. All four bullets struck the pope; two of them lodged in his lower intestine while the other two hit his left index finger and right arm. John Paul, critically wounded, collapsed into the arms of his secretary.

Chaos ensued. The pilgrims mobbed the gunman until the Swiss Guards could get him. He was an escaped convict from Turkey—Mehmet Ali Ağca—a murderer and member of a militant fascist group. He would give multiple stories for why he did it, but the most credible theory is that he was hired by the Soviets. From his planning and travel before the assassination attempt, it was clear he didn't act alone, and he was in contact with Bulgarian intelligence. The Bulgarians very often did Moscow's dirty work. The KGB may not have hired Mehmet directly, but everyone in Poland, probably everyone in the world, believed this was the Soviets striking back.

John Paul was gravely wounded. But despite the near point blank shots from a trained killer, he would live. As he recovered in Rome's Gemelli Hospital, he pondered the significance of the date.

John Paul already had a strong devotion to Our Lady of Fatima. He knew what feast day it was, and so he asked that the third part of the Fatima secret be brought to him. This part of the secret, which Lucia had written down and placed in a sealed envelope in 1944, had only ever been read by a handful of people, including Pope Paul VI, who had read it and returned it to the Vatican Archives without making known its contents. At this point, John Paul had no idea what the envelope contained.

We can imagine what he might have felt when he read of the children's vision of the "bishop in white" being shot. He spent the next weeks and months reviewing the details of what happened at Fatima, meditating on its meaning. He also spoke to the visionary, Sister Lucia, who was still alive.

John Paul became convinced that Mary had guided the bullet so that it would not kill him. "One hand fired the bullet," he would

ABOVE
On the anniversary of
the attempt on his life,
John Paul placed the
assassin's bullet in
Our Lady's crown.

say. "Another hand guided it." As a show of thanks, he took the
bullet and went on a pilgrimage to Fatima the next year, on the
anniversary of the attempt on his life, where he placed it in Our
Lady's crown.

But he knew this wasn't just about his own relationship with
the Mother of God. This was a story that concerned the whole
of humanity.

TRIUMPH OF THE IMMACULATE HEART

John Paul saw the world as a cosmic drama, a struggle between good and evil. From the circumstances of each individual life, to the massive stage of global politics, it was all caught up in God's plan of salvation.

The events surrounding his attempted assassination, with its clear connections to the events at Fatima, proved to be the pivotal and defining moment of his papacy. After that spring day, John Paul became a man on a mission to win the world for his mother's Immaculate Heart.

He reflected above all on the Virgin's request to consecrate Russia to her Immaculate Heart. He was convinced this was the answer to world peace, to avoiding nuclear war and setting millions of people behind the Iron Curtain free. But this consecration was easier said than done. It had already proved to be a difficult task for his predecessors.

Our Lady had requested through Lucia that the pope consecrate Russia to her together with all the bishops of the world. Pius XII was the first to try to heed this request in 1942. By then, World War II was already underway, and he hoped the war would be shortened and its effects lessened through the consecration. While the consecration was well intentioned, it was not made in union with the bishops. Also, he consecrated the world, not Russia, which was contrary to the words of Our Lady.

Pius XII tried again in 1952, this time specifically mentioning Russia, but again he did not do so in unison with the bishops. John XXIII and Paul VI were also unable to fulfill Our Lady's request.

John Paul was determined to make the consecration happen, to do it the right way. But he struggled too. There were enormous logistical, ideological, and political difficulties associated with the task. Millions of Catholics were living under Communist control. To consecrate Russia to Mary could put them in grave danger. Imagine today if the pope tried to consecrate the Middle East to

Mary; there would be a backlash from the Islamic world. This was the sort of risk John Paul faced. But he would not be deterred.

A week after the attempt on his life, Pope John Paul II renewed his own personal consecration to Mary, a consecration he had made in his youth. A month later, he prayed the Act of Consecration for the world and for Russia; but without the bishops, it did not fulfill the request.

He would make the attempt again in May of 1982 on his pilgrimage to Fatima, but his written requests to the bishops to join him were delayed, precluding their involvement. Again, the consecration was a failure.

On his third attempt, John Paul would not fail. He spent three months in preparation. He ensured all the bishops were on the same page, he had the statue of Our Lady of Fatima flown to Rome, and he involved the patriarchs of the Orthodox Church. Two hundred thousand people gathered in St. Peter's Square as he finally, in union with the bishops of the world, fulfilled the request of Our Lady, consecrating the world and Russia to her Immaculate Heart. It was March 25, 1984, the feast of the Annunciation.

Some argued the consecration still wasn't valid because he had not explicitly and audibly mentioned Russia. But he had said "In a special way we entrust and consecrate to you those individuals *and nations* that in particular need to be thus entrusted and consecrated," and he was quick to make clear Russia was a part of the consecration. Shortly after the consecration, Lucia herself confirmed that this finally fulfilled Our Lady of Fatima's request.

Our Lady of Fatima had promised that, in the end, her Immaculate Heart would triumph. On this day in 1984, her promise was fulfilled.

Within a few years of the 1984 Consecration, Communism unraveled. Gorbachev came to power and introduced sweeping reforms that set off the downfall of the Soviet Union, and he acknowledged Christianity's role in Russian history, thereby legitimizing its public practice once again. The Solidarity Movement picked up momentum in Poland, sending over two hundred members to parliament in 1989. The USSR withdrew from Afghanistan. The Baltic republics of Estonia, Latvia, and Lithuania held protests that paved the way for independence. The Soviet navy suffered a devastating accidental munitions explosion at Severomorsk on, oddly enough, May 13, 1984, and now the whole Soviet military began to retrench and cut back. Reformers in Hungary and Czechoslovakia came to power, ousting Communist leaders. Communism was crumbling, and in 1989, its toppling would be complete with the fall of the Berlin wall.

Lech Walesa famously said that the defeat of Communism was a success with many fathers, but that it was impossible not to bow, as a dutiful son, before the paramount champion of the cause of freedom. He was speaking, of course, of John Paul.

In his humility, the Polish pontiff would pass on the credit to his heavenly mother, the same mother who had watched over him as a boy and saved his life in the spring of 1981.

THE DRAGON NEVER SLEEPS

When the Angel of Peace visited Lucia, Jacinta, and Fernando, he told them the hearts of Jesus and Mary had designs of mercy on them. These plans of mercy were not just for the children but for the whole world. How else can we explain the sudden bloodless collapse of a hostile superpower, one that had kept its people imprisoned behind an Iron Curtain? One that propagated atheism and pushed the world to the brink of nuclear war?

The apparitions at Fatima and the consecration of the world to Mary's Immaculate Heart was yet another stage in the battle between Mary and the prince of darkness. Just as she had done at so many other critical periods of history, she intervened to crush the serpent and call us back to her Son.

EPILOGUE

Slithering Through History

LEFT
The devil is the
ancient serpent,
and he moves as a
serpent, making it
difficult to guess
his next move.

From the very beginning, the devil has attacked humanity; but for all his diabolical intelligence and power, he cannot withstand the Woman. We have seen how, across the generations, the Queen of Heaven has protected her children from his assaults, whatever forms they have taken: human sacrifice and pagan worship; revolutions that attacked the Church; persecution and heresies that threatened the truth; global wars; and atheistic empires.

But in following this generational battle, there is one thing we should note about the devil's tactics: *They are constantly changing.* He is the ancient serpent, and he moves as a serpent, snaking this way and that, zigging and zagging, making it ever-difficult to guess his next move. Snakes move unlike any other creature, shunning the natural logic that the shortest distance between two points is a straight line. Yet they are quick and agile, striking their prey like lightning, refusing to allow anything—or anyone—they target to get away. The most fearsome snake who hunts us—the serpent—seems to be always one step ahead. In each century, he has slithered left when we looked right, and right when we heard his hissing coming from the left. With the benefit of hindsight, we can surmise how he has used various movements, ideologies, and even empires as his proxies. But virtually no one notes these movements and ideologies as works of the devil *before* they infect the world with their venom. Often, when we finally make sense of them, it is too late.

So which way has the serpent slithered in this age?

THE TWO-HEADED BEAST

Polycephaly is the condition of having more than one head. A more familiar term might be Siamese twins, or conjoined twins. The phenomenon is extremely rare, but it can happen in both humans and animals. Interestingly enough, polycephaly is most commonly found in one species of the animal kingdom: *snakes.*

In a speech given in 2015, Cardinal Robert Sarah of Guinea highlighted the great evils of our modern times, focusing on two in particular: atheistic secularism and violent Islamic fundamentalism. He called them twin "demonic" and "apocalyptic beasts." Perhaps it is fitting, then, that snakes most often display the phenomenon of polycephaly, for in this age we see the serpent striking at us through two distinct heads.

Today, the most sensational and visible threat to Christians worldwide is the violent attacks of radical Islam. Since it emerged in the seventh century, Islam has been a source of conflict with the Church at many points in history, conquering ancient Christian lands and threatening the heart of Christendom itself at places such as Tours and Lepanto and Vienna. At other times, conflict between the Church and Islam has been supplanted with fruitful dialogue and exchange, founded on a common belief in the "God of Abraham" and desire to obey the will of God; no doubt a relationship of peaceful exchange is the desire of most Muslims. Yet radical Islamists and jihadists are a growing movement and have a different desire altogether: to kill or convert or banish Christians from their lands, to "dechristianize" their territories, and eventually the world, just as the French Revolutionaries and Portuguese masons had attempted, using terror and torture and televised beheadings to accomplish their wicked goals.

While the attacks of radical Islam are apparent and impossible to ignore, a subtler threat is perhaps the more dangerous one: radical secularism. Pope Francis points out that the aim of this movement is "ideological colonization." It is radical secularism that rejects the belief, held not only by the Church but by our founders, that we have a Creator with a plan for his creation—a plan we are not at liberty to tear up or rewrite at whim or will. It is radical secularism that redefines marriage, makes gender a human construct, deems pregnancy not a blessing but a curse, and makes abortion a fundamental human right. It is radical secularism that enshrines these "freedoms"—and sets in its targets anyone who refuses to bow before them.

What a cunning strategy the devil employs in fostering simultaneously both Islamic fundamentalism and radical secularism. These two forces are diametrically opposed to each other in nearly every regard, save one—*their hatred of the Church.*

Radical Islam attacks with the sword and threatens through force; radical secularism attacks with laws and threatens through political correctness. One says you can do no right if your beliefs are too broad; the other says you can do no wrong unless your beliefs are too narrow. One demands total submission; the other, absolute tolerance. One beheads homosexuals and demeans women; the other celebrates homosexuality and belittles men. One allows polygamy and forced marriages and seeks posterity to achieve the victory of the crib; the other prevents children at all costs and murders them when their methods fail.

One says it fights for God; the other fights to remove God.

But despite these contrasting ideologies, they are united in this: both see the Catholic Church as a great hurdle to world domination. They are that two-headed snake that hunts the same prey without realizing they share the same body.

The point here is a simple one. It is not to argue for a moral equivalency between secularism and jihadist terrorism. Still less is it a call to show hatred for ideological opponents, whom the Lord himself commands us to love (Mt 5:44). Rather, it is simply to invite contemplation of the striking fact that two movements that seem on the surface to be such polar opposites, each of whose adherents despise the other, are united by a stronger animus still: hatred of the Catholic Church. This fact suggests these movements are larger than their members, that they are governed or driven by a meta-force, a person or personality that is larger than both, that cares nothing for their aims but only his: to wage war on the Woman and her Son.

How do we evade this predator, this most hideous beast? Hopefully we have learned enough by now that we must, like a frightened child, call out for our mother so she can come and crush the serpent stalking us once again.

THE FATIMA CONNECTION

In Archbishop Sheen's famous book on Mary, *The World's First Love*, already so often quoted in these pages, he devotes an entire chapter to the premise that Mary will be the means by which the Muslims come to Christ.[9]

Sheen begins by noting, as many have before, Muslims have a great respect for Mary, believing in her immaculate conception and the virgin birth. Sheen also points out that the Qur'an has verses on the Annunciation, Visitation, and Nativity. One passage has angels telling her, "Oh Mary, God has chosen you and purified you, and elected you above all the women of the earth" (3:42).

The only possible rival to Mary in Islam, says Sheen, is Muhammad's daughter, Fatima, whom he obviously loved dearly. Yet even still Muhammad wrote of Fatima, "Thou shalt be the most blessed of all the women in Paradise, after Mary."

Archbishop Sheen continues, "Since nothing ever happens out of Heaven except with a finesse of all details, I believe that the Blessed Virgin chose to be known as 'Our Lady of Fatima' as a pledge and sign of hope to the Moslem people and as an assurance that they, who show her so much respect, will one day accept her Divine Son, too." He goes on to point out that the town of Fatima in Portugal inherited its name from the daughter of a Muslim chief, who, after her father and his people were driven out, stayed behind and fell in love with a Catholic boy. This young man eventually named the area after her. "Thus, the very place where Our Lady appeared in 1917 bears a historical connection to Fatima the daughter of Mohammed."

---

[9] Venerable Fulton J. Sheen, *The World's First Love* (San Francisco: Ignatius Press, 2015), see chapter 17, "Mary and the Moslems."

Sheen closes out his chapter by claiming that Christian missionaries will see more and more success in converting Muslims if they preach about Mary, especially as Our Lady of Fatima. "Mary is the advent of Christ, bringing Christ to the people before Christ Himself is born. In any apologetic endeavor, it is always best to start with that which people already accept. Because the Moslems have a devotion to Mary, our missionaries should be satisfied merely to expand and to develop that devotion, with the full realization that Our Blessed Lady will carry the Moslems the rest of the way to her Divine Son."

This argument that Mary will be the source of conversion for a people so seemingly unconvertible is steeped in reason, not wishful thinking. It is clearly true that the Muslim people have a profound respect for Mary, and it is hard even for the skeptic to deny the Fatima connection. It seems that if they accept the Virgin Birth, there is a seed of theology that can be watered with our prayer, and soon Our Lady will bring her Son to them. And once in the hands of Christ Jesus, surely he will harness their passion and commitment and use it for good, just as he did with St. Paul, who once also persecuted the Christians.

Let us not forget that Mary saved us once already in dramatic fashion from the threat of Islam at the famous Battle of Lepanto. This time, though, we must pray not for a military victory but for the softening of hearts and conversion to the one true Faith.

BEARING CHRIST AGAIN IN THE PUBLIC SQUARE

Unlike the threat of radical Islam and Mary's connection through Fatima, there is nothing connecting Mary to radical secularism. And there is certainly no foundation of respect for her in secularism's "dogmas" either, as we see in the Qur'an. Secular governments believe more in forcing us to fund taxpayer abortions and recognize pseudo-marriages than in recognizing the Immaculate

Conception and the Virgin Birth. One might be tempted to think, then, that we can convert our Muslim brother before our local politician.

The Church today faces grave and hostile forms of persecution and attempts at ideological colonization, even from historically or nominally Christian countries. But this hostility did not arise spontaneously. It is the product of decades of indifference to God. A man does not wake up one day and become a cold-blooded murderer. He becomes one slowly, through years of feeding his temper and dulling his appreciation for life through various sorts of stimuli, such as violent movies, video games, drugs, and alcohol. This same phenomenon has happened with our society.

The secularist head of the two-headed beast slow-played us, lulling us to sleep with new forms of entertainment that pushed the bounds of decency little-by-little; technology that leads to a life of constant stimulation, driving away time and space for recollection and prayer; and an absolutizing of tolerance, until today we have a culture that admires sexual debauchery, forces us to fund others' birth control, celebrates gay "marriage," tells children they can be whatever gender they please, legally allows the murder of unborn babies, and in general demands that Christ be eradicated from the public square.

Note that all these attacks are aimed at the family. From the very beginning, the serpent targeted marriage and the family. The family is the fundamental building block of a healthy society. But more than that, the family is the means, over generations and generations, through which God brought us the Woman who would bear his Son. And marriage is a sign to us, an image of the union God desires with humanity.

The devil hates the family because he hates the Incarnation. He hates marriage as a sign of God's love for humanity. He hates the fact that men and women, creatures of flesh and blood, can become God's sons and daughters, too.

From the very beginning, God has pointed us to the Woman,

to Mary, as the answer to the devil's hatred. She is still the answer for us today.

It takes generations for the devil to so weaken and deceive a culture that it will call evil good and exchange truth for a lie, and it can take generations to restore a culture to health. We will never change atheistic secularism overnight. But we can, if we turn to Mary and ask her to bear Christ again—this time in the public square rather than an abandoned cave—bring him to us over time.

Don't forget that she has done this before. Recall that the aim of the state during the French Revolution was to eradicate the Church, to "dechristianize" society. Yet Mary came to a humble little girl and completely changed France's trajectory from a hostile power that persecuted and mocked the Faith to a nation that reclaimed its roots as the eldest daughter of the Church.

Consider too that the Aztecs once sacrificed one out of every five newborns to their pagan gods, but Our Lady of Guadalupe conquered those gods and set those children free. She can no doubt set us free from our own infanticide, too. This is why she is the patroness of the unborn. A beautiful artistic depiction of Our Lady of Guadalupe shows her lifting up an innocent child into the clouds where angels await, saving him from the grasp of the roaring dragon who prowls below. She lifted up the Aztec children in this way long ago, and she will lift up our own.

Finally, consider Our Lady's victory over the largest and most menacing empire the world has ever known: the Soviet Union. At least twelve million Christians were killed because of Soviet atheist policies, while hundreds of millions more lived with the daily knowledge of its hostility to God and its ability to annihilate its opponents with its nuclear forces. Yet at Fatima, the Queen of Heaven came to promise that if we entrusted ourselves, and Soviet Russia, to her, she would convert the atheistic empire and bring peace. Just years after St. John Paul II made this act of entrustment, or consecration, the Soviet Union was in shambles, its iconic symbol, the Berlin Wall, crumbled without a shot.

IN SEARCH OF PEACEFUL SHORES

The serpent knows his time grows shorter as we approach the Last Day when Christ will return. Our ancient enemy is frantic and anxious, eager to corrupt as many souls as he can before suffering his own final defeat. In truth, he attacks with more than just these two beasts; perhaps it is as many as seven heads, as we see in Revelation (see 12:3), no doubt a subtle nod to the seven deadly sins, which if we are being honest, live inside all of us.

But no matter his tactics, no matter how many heads he has or which way he slithers about, we must turn again to our Mother to seek protection and consolation. We must take refuge in her Immaculate Heart, which she promised would never abandon us. For in the sweet embrace of her heart we will forever and always be protected from the attacks of the evil one and come to know the love and mercy of her Son.

So many saints compared Mary to the moon, for she reflects the light of Christ to us when we are lost in the darkness of sin. And just as the moon controls the tides, it is through calling out to the Queen of Heaven that we will turn back the tide of violence, immorality, and corruption, revealing the long-forgotten shores of peace, purity, and humility, allowing us to frolic like children with the One she always leads us back to. Rest assured our Mother will be smiling as she watches from the dunes.

TO THE QUEEN OF HEAVEN

*Have this mind among yourselves, which was
in Christ Jesus, who, though he was in the form
of God, did not count equality with God a thing
to be grasped, but emptied himself, taking the
form of a servant, being born in the likeness
of men.*

Philippians 2:5–7

This, Lady, is your age. The whole court wears
your livery. Every tongue bears praises for
your name. Prayers soar to you in flocks, imploring
your delivery. Your virtue commandeers
the strings of every minstrel. Champions vie
once more to bring you fame. Servants convene
to pay you homage, while learned scholars try
to fathom what it means to call you Queen.

All these honors I affirm. Yet Lady,
I praise this most: that you deem them
    not something to be grasped
But rather welcome, with sweet gentility,
even those whose royal etiquette has lapsed.
For though Queen, you are handmaid still,
    ever drawing near
To every heart that holds the Father dear.

RR

SUGGESTED READING

Fr. Pascale Parente. Angels: *In Catholic Teaching and Tradition.* Charlotte, NC: TAN Books, 1973.

Venerable Maria of Agreda. *The Mystical City of God: A Popular Abridgment.* Charlotte, NC: TAN Books, 2009.

Venerable Fulton J. Sheen. *The World's First Love: Mary, Mother of God.* San Francisco: Ignatius Press, 2015.

Fr. Mitch Pacwa. *Mary – Virgin, Mother, and Queen: A Bible Study Guide for Catholics.* Fort Wayne, IN: Our Sunday Visitor, 2014.

Scott Hahn. *Hail, Holy Queen: The Mother of God in the Word of God.* New York: Image, 2006.

St. Alphonsus Ligouri. *The Glories of Mary.* Charlotte, NC: TAN Books, 1977.

St. John of the Cross. *Dark Night of the Soul.* Charlotte, NC: TAN Books, 2010.

Fr. Gary Castor. *Mary In Her Own Words: The Mother of God in Scripture.* Cincinnati, OH: Servant, 2006.

Fr. Kevin O'Neil. *The Seven Sorrows of Mary.* Liguori, MO: Liguori Publications, 2008.

Tim Staples. *Behold Your Mother: A Biblical and Historical Defense of Marian Doctrines.* San Diego: Catholic Answers Press, 2014.

Rev. Carl G. Schulte, CM. *The Life of Sr. Marie de Mandat-Grancey & Mary's House in Ephesus.* Charlotte, NC: TAN Books, 2011.

Fr. Francis J. Ripley. *Mary, Mother of the Church.* Charlotte, NC: TAN Books, 2009.

Francis Johnston. *The Wonder of Guadalupe.* Charlotte, NC: TAN Books, 2011.

Paul Badde. *Maria of Guadalupe: Shaper of History, Shaper of Hearts.* San Francisco: Ignatius Press, 2009.

Carl Anderson and Eduardo Chavez. *Our Lady of Guadalupe: Mother of Civilization of Love.* New York: Doubleday Religion, 2009.

Abbe Francois Trochu. *Saint Bernadette Soubirous: 1844-1879.* Charlotte, NC: TAN Books, 2012.

Fr. James Martin. *Lourdes Diary: Seven Days at the Grotto of Massabielle.* Chicago: Loyola Press, 2006.

Joan Carroll Cruz. *See How She Loves Us: 50 Approved Apparitions of Our Lady.* Charlotte, NC: TAN Books, 2012.

Fr. Andrew Apostoli. *Fatima for Today: The Urgent Marian Message for Hope.* San Francisco: Ignatius Press, 2012.

Francis Johnston. *Fatima: The Great Sign.* Charlotte, NC: TAN Books, 1980.

St. Louis de Montfort. *Secret of the Rosary.* Charlotte, NC: TAN Books, 1987.

Fr. Michael Gaitley, MIC. *The Second Greatest Story Ever Told.* Stockbridge, MA: Marian Press, 2015.

Peggy Noonan. *John Paul the Great: Remembering a Spiritual Father.* New York: Viking Penguin, 2005.

George Weigel. *Witness to Hope: The Biography of Pope John Paul II.* New York: Harper Collins, 1999.

St. Louis de Montfort. *True Devotion to Mary.* Charlotte, NC: TAN Books, 2010.

Fr. Marie-Dominique Philippe, OP. *The Mysteries of Mary: Growing in Faith, Hope, and Love with the Mother of God.* Charlotte, NC: TAN Books, 2011.

IMAGE CREDITS

Cover The Virgin Annunciate, Batoni, Pompeo Girolamo (1708-87) (after) / Private Collection / Photo © Bonhams, London, UK / Bridgeman Images

Pgs. I, VII, 14-15, 28-29, 42-43, 56-57, 70-71, 90-91, 106-107, 120-121, 136-137, 152-153, 173 Stars at night ©natalia_maroz, Shutterstock

Pg. III Coronation of the Virgin (oil on canvas), Reni, Guido (1575-1642) / Musee Bonnat, Bayonne, France / Bridgeman Images

Pgs. V, 7, 21, 35, 49, 63, 83, 99, 113, 129, 145, 163 Monogram of the Blessed Virgin Mary © germip, Shutterstock

Pg. IV The Virgin with Angels, 1900 (oil on canvas), Bouguereau, William-Adolphe (1825-1905) / Musee de la Ville de Paris, Musee du Petit-Palais, France / Bridgeman Images

Pg. VI The Virgin of the Apocalypse, Miguel Cabrera (Public domain), via Wikimedia Commons

Pg. VIII The Coronation of the Virgin, c.1440 (tempera on panel) (central detail of 49984), Angelico, Fra (Guido di Pietro) (c.1387-1455), Restored Traditions

Pg. X The Empyreum is the final destination in the Divine Comedy of Dante Alighieri (c.1265-1321), at which the traveller enters into the presence of God

Pg. 3 The Fall of the Rebel Angels, 1562 (oil on panel), Bruegel, Pieter the Elder (c.1525-69) / Musees Royaux des Beaux-Arts de Belgique, Brussels, Belgium / Bridgeman Images

Pg. 4 The Marriage at Cana, 1819 (oil on canvas), Schnorr von Carolsfeld, Julius (1794-1872) / Hamburger Kunsthalle, Hamburg, Germany / Bridgeman Images

Pg. 5 Adoration of the Magi, 1423 (tempera on panel), Fabriano, Gentile da (c.1370-1427) / Galleria degli Uffizi, Florence, Italy / Bridgeman Images

Pg. 6 Ms 65/1284 f.64v Fall of the Rebel Angels, from the 'Tres Riches Heures du Duc de Berry' (vellum), French School, (15th century) / Musee Conde, Chantilly, France / Bridgeman Images

Pg. 8 The Celestial Army (oil on panel), Guariento, Ridolfo di Arpo (c.1310-c.1370) / Museo Civico, Padua, Italy / Bridgeman Images

Pg. 10 Satan Vanquished, by Gustave Dore, 1832 - 1883, French. Engraving for Paradise Lost by Milton. 1870, Art, Artist, Romanticism, Colour, Color Engraving, Dore, Gustave (1832-83) / Private Collection / Photo © Liszt Collection / Bridgeman Images

Pg. 12 Madonna and Child (oil on canvas), English School, (18th century) / Erddig, Clwyd, North Wales / National Trust Photographic Library / Bridgeman Images

Pg. 14 Archangel Michael Fights Satan, c.1590 (oil on canvas), Tintoretto, Jacopo Robusti (1518-94) / Gemaeldegalerie Alte Meister, Dresden, Germany / © Staatliche Kunstsammlungen Dresden / Bridgeman Images

Pg. 16 Virgin Mary, Detail From the Annunciation, Masucci, Restored Traditions

Pg. 19 Ms 1476/1943 fol.36v The Woman Clothed with the Sun and the Seven-Headed Dragon, from the 'Hours of Constable Anne de Montmorency' 1549 (vellum), French School, (16th century) / Musee Conde, Chantilly, France / Bridgeman Images

Pg. 20 The Immaculate Conception, 1767-9 (oil on canvas), Tiepolo, Giovanni Battista (Giambattista) (1696-1770) / Prado, Madrid, Spain / Bridgeman Images

Pg. 22 St. Michael Killing the Dragon (oil on panel), Lieferinxe, Josse (Master of St. Sebastian) (fl.1493-1508) / Musee du Petit Palais, Avignon, France / Bridgeman Images

Pg. 24 Detail of a decorative panel showing the Virgin Mary crushing the Serpent, Lamego, Portugal. 1738 (ceramic tiles), Portuguese School, (18th century) / Santuário de Nossa Senhora dos Remédios, Lamego, Portugal / Prismatic Pictures / Bridgeman Images

Pg. 26 Esther Denouncing Haman to King Ahasuerus, 1888 (oil on canvas), Normand, Ernest (1857-1923) / Sunderland Museum & Winter Gardens, Tyne & Wear, UK / Bridgeman Images

Pg. 28 The Last Judgement, detail of Satan devouring the damned in hell, c.1431 (oil on panel), Angelico, Fra (Guido di Pietro) (c.1387-1455) / Museo di San Marco dell'Angelico, Florence, Italy / Bridgeman Images

Pg. 30 Joshua passing the River Jordan with the Ark of the Covenant, 1800 (oil on wood), West, Benjamin (1738-1820) / Art Gallery of New South Wales, Sydney, Australia / Bridgeman Images

Pg. 32 Cain killing his brother Abel, after the painting by Julius Schnorr von Carolsfeld. From Histoire Des Peintres, École Allemande, published 1875 (litho) / Private Collection / Photo © Ken Welsh / Bridgeman Images

Pg. 33 Paradise Lost, 1867 (oil on canvas), Cabanel, Alexandre (1823-89) / Private Collection / Photo © Christie's Images / Bridgeman Images

Pg. 34 The Annunciation, Caravaggio, Restored Traditions

Pg. 36 Annunciatory Angel, 1450-55 (gold leaf and tempera on wood panel) (see also 139312), Angelico, Fra (Guido di Pietro) (c.1387-1455) / Detroit Institute of Arts, USA / Bequest of Eleanor Clay Ford / Bridgeman Images

Pg. 38 Adam et Eve chasses / Photo © CCI / Bridgeman Images

Pg. 40 The Annuciation, La Sueur, Restored Traditions

Pg. 42 Annunciation, Boulogne, Restored Traditions

Pg. 44 The Dormition and the Assumption of the Virgin, c.1430 (gold & tempera on panel), Angelico, Fra (Guido di Pietro) (c.1387-1455) / Isabella Stewart Gardner Museum, Boston, MA, USA / Bridgeman Images

Pg. 47 The Virgin of the Annunciation, 1670-80 (oil on canvas), Murillo, Bartolome Esteban (1618-82) / Museum of Fine Arts, Houston, Texas, USA / Samuel H. Kress Collection / Bridgeman Images

Pg. 48 Pieta, 1876 (oil on canvas), Bouguereau, William-Adolphe (1825-1905) / Private Collection / Photo © Christie's Images / Bridgeman Images

Pg. 50 Detail, Jesus Christ on the Mount of Olives, detail of 1762368, Marieschi, Jacopo (1711-1794) / Museo Civico degli Eremitani, Padua, Italy / Cameraphoto Arte Venezia / Bridgeman Images

Pg. 52 The Massacre of the Innocents, detail from panel one of the Silver Treasury of Santissima Annunziata, c.1450-53 (tempera on panel), Angelico, Fra (Guido di Pietro) (c.1387-1455) / Museo di San Marco dell'Angelico, Florence, Italy / Bridgeman Images

Pg. 54 Jesus Among the Doctors, 1862 (oil on canvas), Ingres, Jean Auguste Dominique (1780-1867) / Musee Ingres, Montauban, France / Bridgeman Images

Pg. 56 Our Lady of Sorrows, 1509-1511, central panel of altarpiece from Mother of God church, by Quentin Massys (1466-1530), oil on panel, 171x151 cm / De Agostini Picture Library / G. Dagli Orti / Bridgeman Images

Pg. 58 Madonna of the Book (Tempera and oil on wood panel) c. 1480-81, Botticelli, Sandro (Alessandro di Mariano di Vanni Filipepi) (1444/5-1510) / Museo Poldi Pezzoli, Milan, Italy / Bridgeman Images

Pg. 60 The Procession to Calvary, by Gaspare Landi, 1806 - 1808, 19th Century, oil on canvas, Landi, Gaspare (1756-1830) / Mondadori Portfolio/ Electa/Marco Ravenna / Bridgeman Images

Pg. 62 Madonna in Prayer, c.1640-50 (oil on canvas), Sassoferrato, Il (Giovanni Battista Salvi) (1609-85) / National Gallery of Victoria, Melbourne, Australia / Purchased through the NGV Foundation / assistance from James O. Fairfax AO, Life Benefactor, 2002 / Bridgeman Images

Pg. 64 Angels, 1895 (oil on panel), Strudwick, John Melhuish (1849-1937) / Private Collection / Photo © Christie's Images / Bridgeman Images

Pg. 67 The Flight into Egypt (oil on canvas), Gerome, Jean Leon (1824-1904) / Private Collection / Photo © Whitford & Hughes, London, UK / Bridgeman Images

Pg. 68 Presentation at Temple, 1808, by Vincenzo Camuccini (1771-1844), Church of San Giovanni in Canale, Piacenza, Emilia-Romagna. Italy, 19th century. / De Agostini Picture Library / A. Dagli Orti / Bridgeman Images

Pg. 70 St. Therese of Lisieux (1873-97) c.1895 (b/w photo), French School, (19th century) / Bibliotheque Nationale, Paris, France / Bridgeman Images

Pg. 72 Christ taking Leave of his Mother (engraving), English School, (19th century) / Private Collection / © Look and Learn / Illustrated Papers Collection / Bridgeman Images

Pg. 75 The Virgin of Calvary, 1861 (oil on canvas), Lenepveu, Jules Eugene (1819-98) / Musee des Beaux-Arts, Nantes, France / Bridgeman Images

Pg. 76 The Madonna of the Magnificat, detail of the Virgin's face and crown, 1482 (tempera on panel) (detail of 9614), Botticelli, Sandro (Alessandro di Mariano di Vanni Filipepi) (1444/5-1510) / Galleria degli Uffizi, Florence, Italy / Bridgeman Images

Pg. 81 Pieta, 1587-97 (oil on canvas), Greco, El (Domenico Theotocopuli) (1541-1614) / Private Collection / Bridgeman Images

Pg. 82 Pentecost by Giovanni Lanfranco (1582-1647), oil on canvas, 373x241 cm, 1630 / De Agostini Picture Library / A. Dagli Orti / Bridgeman Images

Pg. 84 Angel Holding an Olive Branch (oil on panel), Memling, Hans (c.1433-94) / Louvre, Paris, France / Bridgeman Images

Pg. 86 Promulgation of the Dogma of the Immaculate Conception, 1859-1861, Francesco Podesti, Room of the Immaculate Conception, Vatican Museum (photo) / Godong/UIG / Bridgeman Images

Pg. 88 The Marriage of the Virgin, c.1339-42 (tempera on panel), Daddi, Bernardo (fl.1327-d.1348) / Royal Collection Trust © Her Majesty Queen Elizabeth II, 2017 / Bridgeman Images

Pg. 90 Madonna of the Rosary (Cingoli Altarpiece), 1539 (canvas), Lotto, Lorenzo (c.1480-1556) / Mondadori Portfolio/Electa/Antonio Quattrone / Bridgeman Images

Pg. 92 Detail of upper part of Our Lady of Peace by Bernardino Pinturicchio (circa 1452-1513), oil on panel / De Agostini Picture Library / A. de Gregorio / Bridgeman Images

Pg. 95 Pentecost, 16th century, Portuguese painting / De Agostini Picture Library / G. Dagli Orti / Bridgeman Images

Pg. 96 Madonna of the Rosary, Chambers, Restored Traditions

Pg. 98 The Virgin of Guadalupe (oil on canvas), Mexican School, (18th century) / Private Collection / Photo © Christie's Images / Bridgeman Images

Pg. 100 Angel Weighing a Soul, 1348-54 (oil on panel), Guariento, Ridolfo di Arpo (c.1310-c.1370) / Museo Civico, Padua, Italy / Bridgeman Images

Pg. 101 Storming of the Teocalli by Cortez, Emanuel Leutze [Public domain], via Wikimedia Commons

Pg. 103 Aztec Priest Holding Heart from Human Sacrifice, 1892 (engraving), American School, (19th century) / Private Collection / Photo © GraphicaArtis / Bridgeman Images

Pg. 104 The Miracle of the Little Spring, Rafael Ximeno y Planes (Public domain), via Wikimedia Commons

Pg. 106 Photo Our Lady of Guadaulpe © Laksen / Dreamstime.com

Pg 110 First miracle of Virgin, healing of Indian, detail from Miracle of Virgin of Guadalupe, painted by unknown 17th-century artist, Mexico / De Agostini Picture Library / G. Dagli Orti / Bridgeman Images

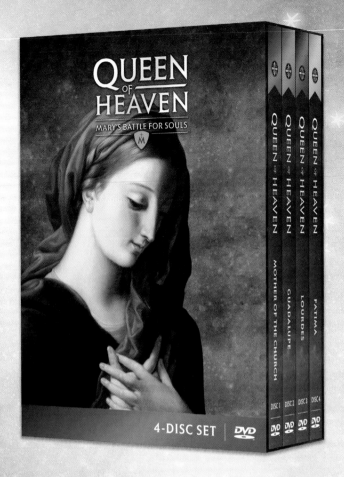

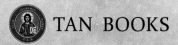